1,000,000 Books
are available to read at

Forgotten Books

www.ForgottenBooks.com

Read online
Download PDF
Purchase in print

ISBN 978-1-330-90640-8
PIBN 10119737

This book is a reproduction of an important historical work. Forgotten Books uses state-of-the-art technology to digitally reconstruct the work, preserving the original format whilst repairing imperfections present in the aged copy. In rare cases, an imperfection in the original, such as a blemish or missing page, may be replicated in our edition. We do, however, repair the vast majority of imperfections successfully; any imperfections that remain are intentionally left to preserve the state of such historical works.

Forgotten Books is a registered trademark of FB &c Ltd.
Copyright © 2018 FB &c Ltd.
FB &c Ltd, Dalton House, 60 Windsor Avenue, London, SW19 2RR.
Company number 08720141. Registered in England and Wales.

For support please visit www.forgottenbooks.com

1 MONTH OF FREE READING

at

www.ForgottenBooks.com

By purchasing this book you are eligible for one month membership to ForgottenBooks.com, giving you unlimited access to our entire collection of over 1,000,000 titles via our web site and mobile apps.

To claim your free month visit: www.forgottenbooks.com/free119737

* Offer is valid for 45 days from date of purchase. Terms and conditions apply.

English
Français
Deutsche
Italiano
Español
Português

www.forgottenbooks.com

Mythology Photography **Fiction** Fishing Christianity **Art** Cooking Essays Buddhism Freemasonry Medicine **Biology** Music **Ancient Egypt** Evolution Carpentry Physics Dance Geology **Mathematics** Fitness Shakespeare **Folklore** Yoga Marketing **Confidence** Immortality Biographies Poetry **Psychology** Witchcraft Electronics Chemistry History **Law** Accounting **Philosophy** Anthropology Alchemy Drama Quantum Mechanics Atheism Sexual Health **Ancient History** **Entrepreneurship** Languages Sport Paleontology Needlework Islam **Metaphysics** Investment Archaeology Parenting Statistics Criminology **Motivational**

Brinton

BEHOLD THE WOMAN,

BEING A SEQUEL

TO "MAN IS LOVE,"

AND COMPANION TO

ECCE HOMO.

I, the Poet, was in the Spirit, on a Resurrection Day, May 30, 1880.

BEHOLD THE WOMAN.

PARABLE SEQUEL TO

MAN IS LOVE.

BY

BULAH BRINTON.

Light, light! more light.
—Victor Hugo.

The soul is a god in exile.
—M. Aurelius Antoninus.

The eyes are the winodws of the soul and bring the most dirrect message from it.
—George Eliott.

Entered according to Act of Congress, in the year 1886, by

BAY VIEW HERALD PUBLISHING CO.,

In the Office of the Librarian of Congress at Washington.

PRINTED BY
D. B. STARKEY & CO, 90 MASON STREET,
MILWAUKEE, WISCONSIN.

To the Happy People of the
NEW HEAVEN
and the
NEW EARTH,
That they may Herein see Through
what Anguish the
God in Exile
Has Passed in the Dreary Pilgrimage
of Life, That they may See the
DIVINE WOMAN,
so Long Covered with the Clouds of
Ignorance, and Only at Last
rescued by the Love of the
DIVINE MAN
To wear the Crown—In the Hope that in the
Physical Changes which will Mark the Entrance of the Race Upon the Life of
the Future, this Record of Travil
and Death, for the Birth and

BEHOLD THE WOMAN.

CANTO I.

THE POET'S STORY.

I, the poet, was in the the spirit on a resurrection day (May 30, 1880.) The veil of nature transparent as clear water. I could see what was, what is and what shall be, for Time and Space were Now and Here. I saw the Son of Man coming in the glory of the rising sun; his form fresh with the dew of the morning flowers. He beckoned me to follow him and I did so, not knowing whither the way or what the object of the journey. Now he showed me a trinity of Spirit, Substance, Space. Each atom or part had the same nature as the whole, so was each atom eternal and indivisible; far Spirit was the life of Substance and Space was the union and separation of each. Now He gave me a chain called Induction, each end being lost in the Infinite. When I measured it I found each link had two sizes, the lesser connected with the end lost on the limit of thought beyond the microscope. The greater with the end lost on the boundary of thought beyond the telescope. Now I saw as the Spirit within Substance moved it took on form. Atom was drawn to atom and I beheld a globe, Earth being its name. Then the Spirit in the ground moved upon the Substance covering the globe with vegetation. And the Life in it took on new form, filling the earth with animals, the sea with fish, the air with birds. The trinity that includes all that is was called God. The trinity that is lost on the boundary of thought was called Atom.

And God said: "We will have children." Now was found latent in all Spirit a germ of life called Soul. Now I saw as the spirit of the living God moved within this seed or germ was born an animal, like, yet unlike, all others. And the name of this being is Man. Now in this being I saw one named Morality. The name of his father was Sin, or transgression of law, and his mother's name was Holiness, or obedience to law.

As I steadfastly gazed upon Nature I saw the law of all was from the single to the complex, from the simple to the compound. Man was an epitome of all, was in the Atom and the living God. Now as he had two natures there was constant strife between the two, and the new creation appeared as a beautiful woman crowned with thorns. And in this crown was the lion's paw, the serpent's teeth, the eagle's talons, also—Death.

And as I listened was heard angels voices proclaiming: "The marriage of the Son, heir of the living God, has come, and his bride will be chosen. Whosoever is worthy to win his love shall wear the Triple Crown and reign with him forever." Then passed before the azure throne all the King's daughters, Jupiter with rolling worlds, Saturn with rings of rosy light, and lovely Venus, pride of the morning and evening. The Son saw but loved them not. A low sad wail of sorrow fills the air. From out the clouds of sense, conceled within a form of flesh, a lovely maiden comes, a crown of thorns upon her brow, and in her hand an empty cup. The heart of·the Son took fire and He loved the beautiful woman whose sorrow He would fain bear. So He took the crown of thorns from her fair brow and did wear it in her stead. Upon her finger He put a betrothal ring, having on the inside the letters S. A. L. V. A. T. I. O. N. Now was the woman very happy in this love, and so did her joy shine through her transparent face that she fled to the wilderness to hide herself.

Now come to her one having the appearance of an angel of light, and spoke thus:

"All hail fair maid I wish you much joy."

"Who art thou?" asked the woman.

"I am the god of Love, servent and friend of thy beloved, who hath sent me to bring to thee this elixir of life, who drinks hath immortal youth and divine beauty," he then placed the cup before her.

"Nay, nay," said the happy woman, "I will take nothing but from the hand of my beloved himself."

"And what wilt thou take to him?" asked the god of Love. "Hath he not left thy cup empty that thou might bring him a drink worthy of the gods?"

"I should be so glad to please Him," she said, and she took the tempting draught.

E'en as she tasted new life and joy distilled in every vein.

She called to her beloved that she might give him also a part. But it came to pass that while her Lord came darkness was over her spirit.

The poison in the elixir went through her blood and turned her happiness into woe. So when her Lord came she knew him not, but spit upon him and thrust a spear into his side. But now as the warm blood from his heart did touch her eyes they opened, and she saw it was her Lord she had slain. So terrible was the sight it broke her heart and her blood flowed out with the life of her Lord. Now from this purple flood there arose a woman fair as the moon, crowned with the stars and spires, mighty as a host of heaven—The Church.

So it was that fallen Earth went through the mysterious depths of Hades that she might find the true exilir of life, which would restore the life of her Beloved. Now when she heard this elixir was only generated in the tooth of the serpent she did gladly open her breast to the serpent, as the mother to her child.

And it came to pass as she was bitten her blood was like unto liquid fire. In her wild frenzy of pain she looked for a deliverer. But instead she saw a wretched man calling vainly upon a friend accross an impassable gulf to bring him a drop of water to cool his burning tongue. And she said, "I can not see a man suffer as I do, so of myself, I will make a bridge across the gulf, that they may bring the water of life from the other side."

Then was the All-Parent pleased and said, "Let the bridge be immortal, and it shall be called Woman's Love."

Now when the poison in her blood had wrought out the death of sin there appeared a new and glorified Life, so was there great rejoicing through all the universe.

Again was heard voices crying through all the realms of Space: "The marriage of the glorified Son has come. Lo! hath he hidden himself and who hath the key to his secret hidding place shall be his Bride and wear the Triple Crown."

Through the smoke of burning insense was seen a queenly One. She was clothed in the regal robes, which only the Kings daughters may wear. In her left hand she carried a roll—the Law. In her right hand the key of the temple. She went in and sought diligently in every part thereof, but she could not find the Bridegroom.

Now was there seen an immense procession. They sang a sweet and solemn chant. The robes they wore showed royal birth and divine majesty. In the left hands of this mighty host was carried a cross. In the right hands the key to saintship.

With music, prayer and song, with insense of fasting and service did the noble Queen of this heavenly host seek Earth's Bridegroom. But her key did not fit his secret hidding place, and so she could not find him.

Now came one born of this world of the senses. Had nought of royal beauty or glory. In her left hand she had a pair of balances, over which hung a glittering steel. In her right hand she carried the key of the world's storehouse of wisdom and knowledge. Earnestly through all her vast dominion did she seek the Son. But alas she could not find him. Neither miscroscope, telescope, magnet or steel would reveal his secret hidding place.

And I wept bitter tears of disappointment, so much did I desire to see Earth's glorfied Lord.

CANTO II.

THE NEW LIGHT.

Now it came to pass as my tears made a new transparent atmosphere, I saw a temple of seven priests. In the left hand of each priest was a light of exceeding brightness. With the right did each point the people to the way of holiness, which leads to the kingdom of God.

And it came to pass as they ministered around the alter there came a breath from the realm of darkness which put out all their lights except a spark in the center of the alter. Now while the people were in this thick darkness there came demons of Passion, Appetite, Lust and Selfishness, and these destroyed the people on every side.

But lo! as the cries of the perishing were borne on the wings of the wind they touched the heart of a woman, and she came to the rescue. In her left hand she carried the elixir of life, and in her right a luminous key did shine by the light from within. The bar was flat—substance, onyx. On one side was the mirror of the soul; on the other the words Perfect Love. The letters were of diamonds, clear as the light. The handle was of sapphire with a circle of pearls. On the end was a serpent. Through the transparent coils could be seen the letters S. S. S.

Now was a ditch here where many had fallen. These were wallowing in the mire like swine.

And it came to pass as the light of the woman's key fell

upon one in the ditch, could be seen the mark of the beast on his whole body. So as the woman tried to give him of the elixir he was in great rage like as a mad dog, and sought to bite her. But when she had overcome the beast and opened the door of his heart he was as a lamb.

Then did she hold the mirror of her key before him. What was her joy and surprise to see there the image of her Glorified Lord. This was his secret hiding place. But the Son knew her not. His heart was heavy and sad with grief for the loss of his first betrothed, and he would have none but her for his bride. Now as he fled to the wilderness, where he had last seen her, to weep for her he found there the woman with the luminous key.

As she held up her hand he saw on the ring the shining letters S. A. L. V. A. T. I. O. N. How now did his heart leap for joy and gladness as he said: "Ask now what ye will and I will give it you."

And she said: "May it please my Lord to give each person in the prison of the flesh two angels, one for the right side and one for the left. So shall the body no more be a prison for thy children but the place where angels do minister to them."

So was the Lord pleased with her request that He said: "Close now thine eyes."

She did so.

"Kiss now thy right hand and wave towards heaven. Kiss now thy left hand and wave towards earth."

She did so.

"As you have done my darling so may all do. Thus shall the right hand become a cherubim of love to send one's kiss to heaven, the left a seraphim of faith to send one's love and trust to those in the flesh. God will answer by sending the heavenly doves to the heart."

CANTO III.

MARRIAGE OF THE SON.

Now that the Bride was ready the King of Heaven made a marriage feast and sent his angels to the four quarters of the globe to bid the guests come to the banquet. They came from the North, South, East and West. All who had the image of the Son upon their foreheads went in to the supper. Those who had the image of the beast were shut out.

And I, the poet, saw the Son in his glory, and the Bride in her beauty, and so exceeding was the brightness that I became as one sun-blind and I fell to the ground with awe and trembling. Seeing I could not endure the light and glory of their presense the beautiful Bride sent an angel to show me her wedding ring, that I might tell it to her friends.

It was of pure gold, showing the bond of union for all mankind. On the top was a circle of six diamonds of wonderous brilliance. In the center of the circle, as the sun in the center of the stars, was one that exceeded the others as the sun transcends the earth. The name of this was Christ the anointed Son. The names of those in the circle were Abraham, Buddah, Confucius, Zoriaster, Socrates and Mohomet.

As the light of these stones fell upon my eyes instead of dazzeling as the other had done the sight was enlarged. I saw thus a ray of light coming direct from the throne of God, falling upon the heads of men, as the sun's rays upon a prism, this light had become the seven religions of the earth. Now was the light reflected from the Bride's ring, the same pure white light had come first from God.

Filled with surprise I asked the angel: "What is this religion that hath in itself the light of all?"

She put her hand upon my lips to seal with silence. Speak not the unspeakable. Name not the unnameable. But she showed me the wedding present the Lord and his Bride had sent to earth.

'Twas a likeness of the luminous key—perfect love. The mother's was larger than the child's. It was of glass clear as crystal. The bar was a tube into which the mother puts clear water with a crystal of salt every morning. The key is then hung over the family table by a cord of three colors. At the hour of evening devotion the mother spills the water upon the ground, to signify the tears shed by the heart of love for the sins and failures of her children. It is poured on the ground to show that love sends back the sins of her offspring to the dust.

Now it come to pass as the banquet was most perfect in all signs of joy and happiness, when the Lord sought his Bride he found her weeping. He asked thus: "Why weepest thou my Beloved? Have I not given thee all thou wishest?"

She said: "Oh, my Lord! How can I enjoy all this love, light and music when so many of our Father's children dwell in darkness and pain? Hear how their cries of woe mingle with this happy music."

Now as the Lord looked into her eyes and marked how they shone through her tears, she was more lovely and pleasing than ever before. And puting his hand upon her cheek, blessing her tears spake thus: "Henceforth let the sweetest, divinest joy distill in happy tears."

It was done according to his word.

Then gave he command to the angels saying: "Let the music stop, the feast wait, while all the guests follow my Bride and Me into the outer darkness to rescue our brethren therein. For I say unto you all not one shall taste of my supper till he bring some lost one to share it with him."

Upon the head of the Bride was a triple-crown, and her face shone as the sun. As she leaned upon the arm of her Lord, the glory of God the Father and Mother did so shine through them, they must needs put a veil upon their faces. Men saw them thus as light behind a crystal screen.

They first went to the temple of the seven priests, whose lights had gone out. They saw upon the steps of the temple a woman had given herself a burnt offering. Who ceased not to cry unto God night and day in behalf of sin-sick men. Now being in great agony of soul her countenance was as a woman in trial, and she cried out: "Oh God! Father and Mother of all, if one of thy children be lost it shall be me, for I will hold the last one to thy heart till thou dost save from all sin." Then did her spirit go out of her and she fell to the earth as one dead. Her hands were clasped over her brest thus: The right thumb pressed against the left forefinger. The rest following in dove-tail fashion. The left thumb sealing them together with the word Amen. It was two o'clock, P.M., when she prayed thus.

Now as the Lord touched her eyes she saw Him and His beautiful Bride, and in their hearts she could see all mankind purified and saved from sin. And while she spake not for joy the Lord said: "What wilt thou that I do for thee now?"

She said: "Oh, thou eternal Friend, Lover and Saviour

of men, I pray thee light up the torches of the priests in the temple."

And e'en as she spoke the sparks did flame up as the purest electric lights; and the temple was filled with divine glory.

Thus spake the Christ: "Let the hands clasped over the heart, as thine, spell the word *salvation* from this time forth until the light now seen here shall enlighten the whole world."

And commencing at two o'clock P. M. the prayer for the world's salvation followed the course of the sun and thus every moment did the insense of this desire rise to heaven from the hearts of earth's children.

Now when the Christ and his Bride came to the Enchanted Isles, where reigns the Siren Queen, I looked intently to see what they would do for the men who had been enchanted by the Siren's song and then turned into swine. But a mist was on the Isle and I could see nothing distinctly. Near me was a young man whose name is Science. He was trying expeisments with the sun's rays. I said: "Pray throw some of your light upon this isle that I may see what will be done for the victims of the Siren."

"It is all bosh," said the youth, "Science has nothing to do with such folly."

TOM'S STORY.

The fire was burning in the old fashion grate. Again was I a boy with the Rosewell family. Eva was beside me, as in the happy days of youth. My pulse thrilled. She had come to me. But when I reached out my hand to clasp her's it was worse than with Æneas in the shades of the departed. I touched only the impsasive air. I fairly shrieked with the anguish of baffled hope and confidence. All the bright illusions of the past, which had just come to me, were so terrified by the sound, they fled like frigtened ghosts. I was alone.

Eva, you must come to me, or I shall come to you. I could endure your absense if I were perfectly certain of again having you. But these torturing doubts, this answered and yet unanswered question "If one dies shall one live again." I—I—can't endure this longer. If though dead you still live I will find you, though I scale the walls of infinity, though I touch all space. If you are no more, then am I no more—life worse than a delusive dream—I will now end by stopping the cause. My will is signed. Those who earned the property the law calls mine will have it. The last word of my History is written. Now, my darling, have I not a perfect right to give the reins to my heart and let it take me to you, or to eternal nothingness?

All the old time torturing doubts of immortality now

flamed and glowed with the lurid brilliancy of hell, as the hand-writing of doom—eternal loss of Eva. The thought of losing myself did not come to me. It was simply this: She had gone into eternal shade—everlasting nothingness. This thought so pressed my heart as to stifle me. It smothered my breath, as one gasping for air. Should I go out of life thus choked like a criminal? No, I would go as a man, if life is really not worth the living. I went to my desk. The flickering light of the fire fell upon the glistening steel; also upon a work of Buddah. All the horror and dispair pictured upon its pages seemed to burn into my very soul. The worst of all being the idea that the death I was now seeking would bring no relief. Death was but ridding oneself of one curse to become the victim of a greater. It was getting off one wheel to be racked and tortured on a greater and stronger one. This new phase of feeling staid my hand, while I played with this life as the cat with the mouse she has caught. I laid my head upon my right hand, my elbow resting upon my desk. How long I know not. With dispair, as with joy, "time is no more." A vague, misty sense of the presence of Eva came over me. Oh! surely this was too cruel. Why must I always be tortured with these illusive shadows that vanish at the touch of reality, like the mists of morning?

Eva! Eva! if you are here why don't you let me know it? Doubt here is damnation. The mighty energy of my dispair seized the shadow before me and transfixed it to the spot; infused into it substance and made it a palpable reality. It took hold of my hand. I trembled with a new hope. Perhaps as Jesus had taken the hand of Thomas to convince by the power of touch of his identity so she might do for me. At once the scientific spirit of the age replied to my thought. What is this but another illusion caused by the impression that story has left upon the brain? I groaned aloud, and literally fell into a heap of nothingness. What was there in religion, faith or hope but the touch of Science would destroy? I was simply one body of pain. All will power, all motive to contend longer was gone. During all the years since she left me how had I fought to be able to believe in her coming again. All this now seemed to belong to another life. As helpless as an infant of days, I fell at the feet of Love and begged for her, as one begs for life. I now saw a stream of light, like unto a luminous chain ascending and decending from the desk where my hand rested. A form was there. In this light was revealed the hand and arm I had lost at Gettysburg? I thought of the doctrine or Buttler's Analogy, also of Problems of Life, where the teaching is to prove this outer life of flesh but the shell or covering of the real life. Surely this dead hand now seemed the only living thing about me. It actually took the pencil upon my tablet and wrote something. Hope revived, I lived again. I tried to read what my hand had written. But although the light was as bright and clear as the purest electric glow, yet I could not discern even the form of a letter by it. But when at last the light of my lamp fell upon the tablet, what did I see. *Eva's writing*!! It is vain to think what may be the possibilities of eternity. But if there be in store for me anything to exceed the joy of that moment I think I don't want to know it. For devoutly do I wish that this moment may ever stand for me as the highest possibility of my being. Eva still lives—*forever mine.*

Upon the same wave of joy, she sailed outside the boundaries of this life. I should soon have followed her had not the old mocking spirit that always pursued me whispered: "Fooled again with a shadow. Hadn't you better test this wonderful phenomena?" I had not even thought to read the lines. It was her writing, that was enough. She still lived not only to prove immortality but what was more precious to me, the certainty of life. Now I'll try and calm myself and read. "Go to the rock and find my ring." Again the mocker: "This letter is addressed to nobody and signed by nobody. Send for your servants and let them take you to the Asylum at once." Volumes have been written to tell the power of faith but who has ever tried to tell the destructive power of that arch enemy of the race, Unbelief? At the touch of this monster's fingers, at the sound of his mocking voice all that beautiful world wherein I had just found my darling vanished like the light of beauty before the clouds of the cyclone. Would I allow this demon of darkness, who had annihilated God in the minds of so many of his children, to now come and rob me of Eva after I had lost her so long?: No, it should not be so. This power, so long opposed by Faith, should now be confronted in his last stronghold by Fact. So strongly was he entrenched in the outward senses that he must be fought on this ground. The old weapon had become blunt and dull through the conflict of the ages to pierce him. To that stone would I go and there would I find the weapon already forged that would insure me a complete victory. Thus should he loose his deadly grip upon the hearts of Earth's children.

With my fleetest horse I had time to reach the morning train, which would bear me near the spot. It was a question of confidence or despair. If this was from Eva I should find something tangible, for surely she would not trifle with me. But one thing was certain, should this prove a delusion not all that Buddah, Shakespeare or St. John had said about the possibility of something worse beyond this outer life would keep me here one hour after I was convinced that this experience was a delusion of the imagination. So while I gave directions about my horse I looked out for my revolver; had put into my traveling bag all sorts of things needed for digging, testing, etc. One thing more, Mammy had long been in her grave but her pious husband was still with us. His words had once saved me when I was about to be swallowed up in the vortex of passion. I must have his benediction now. As the blind old patriarch laid his hands over me he felt the revolver. "Do massa tink de dear Lord need dis to keep him wid?" he said as a look of pain and reproach came on his black face. That look seemed to pierce all that cloud of sophistry which for years had been hovering over my heart, hiding the light by the conviction that the Stoics were right in the belief that when life was only a burden we had a right to lay it down as a useless weight. I stood now before that honest, brave, old man a convicted coward, thinking to escape a possible pain by the crime of suicide. What an insult to the All-Parent, who had given me life—aye more, had given me Eva. I fell on my knees by that bedside and truly did the Infinite Helper reach out a hand to me, as the old man placed his, on my head uttering the old-time prayer, "Lord bless massa Tom and keep him from de ebil of dis wicked world."

I left my weapon with him and started off with a lighter heart. It would be hard to tell whether I most desired or dreaded the arrival of the train at my destination. The hope this would prove true did so struggle with the doubt of any possibility of confirming the reality of it that I was calm from a simple excess of emotion. The most stupid waiter was not more calm seemingly than I. But when the old familiar scenes were again before me, eager longings broke up this deceptive quiet and threw me into a fever of excitement. By that old stone where I had once found her should I find her again, though in another form? Somehow the touch of the rock gave me strength, and I began to dig around it. Why I did so was a mystery. Surely she was not in that ground nor could she be found by the tests I had with me. I uncovered something shiny. Great Heavens! the very ring I had given her as the seal of our betrothal. She had brought it here the night of the fire and now she would hold it up before me as the visible pledge that though absent from the flesh she was here in another form, just as real, aye more so, because more substantial. One who has reached and passed the highest possibility of rapture can never again reach, much less, transcend it. I was convinced by this new expression that the moment I saw the hand-writing of my Eva was the moment of all time for me. With the ring upon my finger I could live over and over again that blissful moment. Through the medium of the arm I had given my country at Gettysburg Eva had been able to reach me. This did not seem so very strange now that I thought of what I had just read, how a man in the West had been able to discern the lost arm of another by some powerful lens he had constructed for testing the reality of the invisible body, that is developed and produced through the visible. Aye more, he had been able to write with the hand whose covering of skin, bones and muscles had long since decayed. He had been incited to these experiments by the fact of the man suffering so with his lost arm. Surely there must be something there to give him such pain. So had I suffered with mine. If I was certain of feeling such pain through it could I not be equally certain of feeling the thrill of joy that always comes at the touch of her hand? It were just as easy now to convince me I had never felt the pain as that I did not now hold my darling with that same arm. It was the one member of my body in the same state or condition as hers. And it was just like my Eva to clasp this hand, press it to her glorified life, that thus the electric circle so long disturbed by her death might be again put into right conditions, and thus bind us together in a chain death could no more touch. Every part of my invisible body was just as real as the arm from whence the flesh had fallen. I could meet her life with mine. The throbs of her heart found answer in mine, though still veiled with its fleshy covering. By means of that arm I could meet her as in the days when we were both behind the walls of flesh, aye much more perfectly, for did not this dark veil like a thick cloud often and often hide us from each other?

Here she was now in all the freshness and sweetness of her early love, with all the later life had added to her charms and graces. With all the grossness of sense purged away, with all earthy passion transformed and crystalized into the diamond of perfect love, I now received back my Eva after all these years of separation. She was as real as the air I breathed, as impalpable as the electric currents; she moved me just as powerfully. She had by her mighty love conquered all the obstacles of space, all the obstruction of matter and come that she might be all in all to me.

Of course, it could not have been Eva if she had long left me to enjoy her presence without thought of others. Had I needed any further proofs of her identity, of the fact that she was the same girl who had got possession of my youthful affections, had given me the first glimpse of true womanliness, I felt them as she breathed into my ear by a new process of speech: "Why Tom, how selfish we are. How are you going to give this light to those who are in the darkness of doubt and fear? Oh, the selfishness of the flesh. The first law of animal life is self, and we shall never get away from its domination while in the animal form." I said very impatiently: "What do I care for them? Let them struggle to the light as I have. I am going to enjoy you now I've got you back." I suppose being in the spiritual body she could not understand the old language of the flesh. So instead of the grieved look or sharp reproof of the old time, when I had so distressed her by my boyish selfishness, she smiled as sweetly as ever she did, when I had done some hoeric act of self-denial.

She now led me into the family circle; into the invisible world she now lived in. I could see through her eyes, hear with her ears, touch with her hands. Man-like at every step of our progress I must stop and know the cause of the thing I felt, find the law that produced and governed the sensation I was conscious of feeling. Somehow a universe of atoms; each atom comprising a Trinity of Spirit, Substance, Space was shown me. These were continually dissolving in old forms and combining in new. These were inseparable, for Spirit was the life of Substance and Space was both the separation and union of both. Neither could exist without the other.

My darling was the same woman she was before she left me, except that she now lived in a more rarefied form. She had left the crude, fleshy state and now lived in the refined, spiritual state. As light escapes the lump of coal during combustion, so had she escaped through the dissolution of her flesh and was now come to stay with me as she was not permitted to do in the flesh. I thought of Moses forbidden to enter the land of promise in the old form, but in the new could came and talk with the Son on the mountain.

Having thus found a scientific and historical basis for the happiness I felt I allowed her to take me into her world. My hand clasped in hers, everything she felt I could feel, what she saw I saw. It were just as easy to put the thrill of music, the transports of love, the beauty of flowers into novels as my sensations. Why could not it always be thus? Why must she leave me again? One day I was talking to her (of course we spoke the language of the higher life) of the doubts which had so long distracted and pursued me about the reality of her living. "Why Tom," she said, "how many do you suppose are still victims of such unbelief?" "Their name is legion," I said, little thinking how surely I was signing my own warrant of separation. The old light was in her eye, only intensified by the new and higher life she now lived, as she said: "Tom, let us part at once, you go in one direction and I in another and et us search every realm of Fact and Faith until we can bring the light these people need. We read of the Devil appearing as an angel of light, let us make him so in reality. Let us transform these demons of Doubt, Darkness, Despair into a living force to lead men to Light, Liberty and Love." That was Eva's way of beating the Devil. To her he was simply a benighted person seeking light. She never could see anything bad anywhere or in any person. Her nature was like a blue light, making everything blue it touches: There was enough love in her to light up all creation. It was idle to tell her she saw only the reflection of herself in others. Her answer would be: "Oh Tom, if you could only love them as I do you would see them just the same." I had no logic for that sort of argument. I think I must have improved a little during our last interviews for somehow I felt ashamed to urge her from the course she marked out for herself and me. My heart seemed to be filled up with something of the Infinite Pity for those who still suffered as I had. Moreover this new experience had fired anew my youthful enthusiasm to do something grand, good and noble. It had revived or rather resurrected my old confidence that there was some way out of this labyrinth of mystery, would show us a new meaning in life. This seemed possible now that it was so embodied and expressed in her.

The best explanation I can give of the way she appeared now is found in watching the body during the process of cremation. There is a time when the heat has driven all the volatile gases out of the body. It now weighs from five to six pounds. It is perfectly luminous and transparent. The form is exactly as when the body weighed one hundred and fifty pounds. But the earthy substance has been burned and only the pure luminous form remains. A breath of air and this too dissolves, leaving nothing but a handful of dust.

A slight change in the electric currents which had bound us together parted us, and my darling was gone, living only in my life by the change she had wrought in me. The old rock was as bare, the woods as desolate as though my Eva had never visited them. I left that memorable place a changed man. Doubt should now be my good angel to lead me to find the truth of things, Despair the stimulus to prompt to effort, as hunger prompts to effort for the supply of the body's need, the Devil a very useful individual to stir me up with his long stick if I get careless, or to teach me perseverance. Did I see her then? If I do see her before I can lay at her feet the spoils of victory it will be because she seeks me.

CANTO V.

THE FIVE FRIENDS.

*Enter—Poetry, Science, **Wisdom**, History and Ignorance.*

P.—Well friends I have a parable I would like to present to you this morning.

S.—Parables—Nonsense. Science deals with facts.

I.—Parables are like pictures, and I like 'm better nor yer facts.

P.(*aside*)—Whether is this man or woman? Wrinkled with age, tottering and trembling with decay; yet fresh with immortal youth—a face made perfectly charming by childish innocence—an old hag with the sweet face of the cherub babe.

W.—Well Science what is the product of thought but fact? Define thought for us.

S.—Thought is the most perfect manifestation of cosmic force known to us—takes in the whole universe at a glance—condenses all space—takes in the evolved results of time, and sets sail for eternity. Only the extremes of the Infinite can escape its grasp. It is the life-germ of all mach——

W.—That will do. What is a parable but a creation of this wondrous power.

S.—Well to tell the truth I don't want to have anything to do with our friend the Poet just now. She claims to see a world that is best left invisible to me for the present at least. There may come a time for me to enter it, but it is not now. I will keep listening while Wisdom decides those questions which Science has no scales to weigh.

W.—We are to deal with a word painting. Words are of the same nature as water. Under the electric currents of thought they show the same transformation as water, which appears as vapor, steam, fluid or ice.

S.—Give us a test to prove your assertion.

W.—Take the word God. Poet, please tell us what the Hebrew sees in this transparent word.

P.—One Person, Almighty Creator, outside Nature, etc.

W.—Give only the principle object. What does the Pantheist see?

P.—Universal Force immanent in Nature. The efficient cause of all phenomena. The Atheist sees a Nothing.

W.—What does the Positivest see in the same word?

P.—An unknown image of the Unknown and Unknowable.

W.—You have given the extremes now for the shadings. What does the Christian find in the word?

P.—A Trinity of three beings or persons in One. And to fill up the space between these opposites we have every variety of Being or no Being; from a loving Father counting the hair of His children's heads to a mighty man of war destroying His enemies, or consuming His children in everlasting fire. Also a being caring nothing for man or his petty interests and works.

W.—Science, please tell us the cause of the changes we see in a word of but three letters.

S.—The thought of each affects and determines the meaning of the word.

W.—Therefore words can have no unchangeable value or meaning. Being symbols of thought they very with the thought of each person who uses them.

I.—Are ye tr'in' to make out the Bible aint no better nor water?

W.—My dear Ignorance, can anything be better than a fountain of living water. If we can show you the river of life in the book you love, will it not be better than a lot of letters which can be made to spell anything or nothing according to the thought of the reader?

I.—I don't care nothin' about what ye can show me. I was happy and contented before I ever see any of ye. Now I am worried to death with new theories.

S.—Such happiness is not for us. I would like to try an experiment with some phrase—take Son of God. History can tell what has been and what is the effect of thought upon this sentence.

H.—In the infancy of the race it was as natural for men to call themselves sons of God as to call father or mother. After a time men began to deny that others were sons of God. Finally the Hebrews desired to have Jesus crucified because He said He was a son of God. About fifteen hundred years after, one of His friends was burned at the stake by another party of His friends because he said Jesus was the son of God. So it came to pass that in these three words men have found everything from the most sublime truth to the most terrible blasphemy, from soul-saving orthodoxy to soul-destroying heresy. What each person sees in this phrase is largely the creation of his own thought. I find it impossible to explain the record I have made with, or by any other theory.

W.—From such experience embracing the whole history of men, we may formulate the law of words:

RULE I. Words are symbols of thought whose meaning or value is affected by the thoughts they symbolize.

RULE II. Words are living organisms. Hence they

obey the law of growth and decay that is the universal phenomena of all life.

I.—I don't see what's the good of words if a fellow can change 'm 'round anyway.

W.—This law gives each one a chance to put a good meaning in the words one employs. And now having found the changable nature of words, proving them to be good, bad or indifferent, (steam, ice or water) through the influence of thought upon them. Let us test events by the same process. Perhaps we my find good where others have found only evil.

S.—So much attention has been directed to the Cross let us begin with that.

W.—Follow the order of development, as evolution is the law of life, so wait till you come to that. Begin with the first on the ring.

H.—Buddah lived about five hundred years before Jesus. He showed men a religion that is today the faith of one-third the children of men.

P.—Western learning sees in this stupendous fact a religion of negation, entirely without God, Soul or Immortality.

W.—What does Poetry find here?

P.—A God whose existence is a truth both too simple and too sublime and complex to admit of proof. An infinite truth, completing the whole circle; with the Sonship of man in the center. It is a truth weakened by proof, which admits a doubt, as a broken circle. As a planet becomes a comet, doubt affects this truth.

W.—The difference then between Eastern and Western thought is shown by two teachers of geometry. One leads his pupils into elaborate descriptions and demonstrations of the possible existence of a line and a dot. When they have come to a perfect apprehension of this possibility he makes a line and a dot. The other does this at once, and goes on to show his pupils how to solve the problems. Buddah wasted no time constructing water prisons (word definitions) to limit and confine the infinite God.

P.—He did not even give them a word image or any other idol of marble or clay. But having fought his way to the table lands of Nirvanna he pointed the people to the Noble path which would lead them to it—right doing, etc. The eight wonder of the world is that of Western thought fixing itself upon the dead letters of the word "Nirvanna," and utterly blind to the living man right before them. How could Nirvanna be annihilation when there he was, "He who just began to live when he got into it."

W.—A most striking proof of the blindness of word worship. The most ignorant———

I.—Why yes, I'd known better ner that myself. A dead man couldn't be tryin' to help me get religion, or be a nothin', wantin' to git me nowbar.

P.—We find in this religion a glorious proof that we are not obliged to multiply words about God, the Soul, and Immortality. But instead reach out the hand of Love and at once help men on the road that leads unerringly into the Unnamable, the unthinkable.

W.—Starting now from the table lands of morality, whither all the men named in the circle of the ring sought to lead their fellow men, let us ascend to the Cross, and let History tell us what thought has made of this event—the crucifixion of Jesus.

H.—The death of God and the life of man. The death of man and the life of God. Between these opposite poles of thought there is every shade and variation, the words of which have formed a whole ocean; pure water of life to some; a lake of eternal fire; a volcano or mountain of ice to others. The Roman soldiers, who beheld it, stood in awed silence; or with hushed breath declared "surely this is the Son of God."

W.—We can do no better then they. Leaving its unthinkable, unspeakable mysteries to the heart we will try to find the living water flows———

S.—I don't find any pure water of life in it. I see a noble man teaching wondrous truths in much higher and purer form than any of his predecessors. I see him tortured and put to death by his bigoted countrymen. I see the sweetest, most loving words man ever spake tortured and turned into living death and hell for———

I.—I declare I'm sick to death of this everlasting ding-dong about hell, *hell*!! It don't amount to a hill of beans. I just let my youngones say, "Oh God, if there haint no God don't damn our souls if we haint got no souls." They are just as safe then if there haint no God as they are if there is. Folks has got to have somethin' to eat in this world.

S.—A very sensible thing to do. Much wiser than the course of our friend Poetry, who is always stirring people up with questions about which it is impossible to know anything definite. Barren speculations. Look at the East, while dreaming about their souls their bodies have become living skeletons, with the breath of life kept in by the charity of the English, whom science tought how to make this world worth living in and how to make life and———

P.—Dear History, pray tell us the age of our young friend.

H.—Not very old, hardly of age; yet a child of wonderful promise.

I.—Not very old, I should say so. A puking, squalling

baby crawling on all fours. I've seen plenty such brats in my time, as 'twas going to work wonders and drive me out of the universe. But I aint dead yet. No thanks——

W.—Nor likely to be for some time yet. But when our friend Science asserts that nothing can be certainly known of the things the Poet has been showing us, it is an assertion without proof. History will tell us what progress was made in physical science before Bacon showed the right method of discovering truth, thus enlarging continually the realm of the known from the spoils of the unknown.

H.—Nothing worth the name of progress. The inductive method was as the slow moving waters of the lakes drawn into the rapids of Niagra. And yet we are not out of the creeping state. What are the possibilities of progress when science is erect on her feet?

W. Very well. Now if all these marvelous changes owe their origin to the observation of the workings of nature, in earth's changes instead of looking into the mud-pens of thought, called words—stagnant water—whose only life was the result of putrification; what may we not expect when the student of man turns his attention from words to living men; and seeks here the solution of life's problems—the law of his being?

S.—But how is one going to know anything of a world one can neither see, nor hear, nor feel?

W.—Please drop the last word and wait for proof on that point. Because men found nothing but death in the word Nirvanna you have no right to say no life could be found in Buddah. So let us with hope instead of despair begin at the beginning. Follow Goldsmith in his Animated Nature, and observe the child from its first independent existence; succeeding the fact of conception. What do we find here?

S.—A being invisible to the naked eye, but possessed of a force of sufficient power to draw sustenance from all its surroundings, continually dying to live anew until it comes to the full statue of man or woman. After a few years in which the life and death forces balance; are neutral as the gases in water; the death force gains on the life force until with the last breath it is entirely vanquished, as a spark gone out.

W.—At what period of its existence does this being receive the most powerful impressions from outside parties and influences?

S.—During its nine months of fetal life. Not all its three score years and ten can undo the work of this generative period. The seed derived from the parents determines its whole future developments, as certainly as the acorn the oak. This again is slight compared to the impressions made upon its sensative organization through the mother. It can be frightened into idiocy or death by the sights and sounds of war; it can receive marks from every object in nature, from red cherries to white handkerchiefs; it can be frightened into life-long fear of every thing from a mouse to an elephant; it can be made to love or hate its own father; aye it can be guillotined while yet in its mother's womb, as was done in France.

W.—And yet it receives all these impressions from a world it is not born into. Pray tell me then does it know anything of the world outside its own narrow bounderies?

S.—Not through selfconsciousness. This is a flame that only lights up at a later period of growth, sleeps when we sleep, burns low in a fever, in fact is governed entirely by the condition of the brain.

W.—A very uncertain thing truly, as you have shown, the knowledge that affects us most is had without its aid.

The most it seems to do is to localize the power of sensation that is distributed over the whole body when it sleeps, in the nerves of the eyes and ears when it works; so causing us to feel them less powerfully. It is a watch dog that wakes up when it has a chance to bite.

S.—One never knows anything about ones nerves or body until bitten by it. Yet the pain is all in the nerves, like powder in a revolver waiting its touch.

W.—Now Science, may there not be something in this latent pain in the nervous system like the hell of the———

I.—Hell is it? Now who ever heard the beat of that? I never once thought when I heard talk like yourn that you'd fetch up there. Oh, I do wish I could go to sleep.

W.—Well this is getting rather stupid. Will not the Poet enliven us up a little with some of her fancy pictures?

P.—I see a number of persons as nearly like us, as ourselves in miniature. They are enclosed in narrow cells, surrounded by water and enclosed by thick, muscular walls. They are discussing the question of a future life: Resolved That there must be a world outside of this we live in. Poetry took the affirmative while Science led the negative.

Affirmative—There must be something beside this, cause what are we here for? Are we any good to ourselves or anybody else? What's the good of our eyes if we aint ever going to have any light; our lungs if we are never to have any air? Would any sensible person spend his time making such hands as ours if there was nothing for them to do? And who that cared anything for us would make such long legs as ours to be forever cramped up like we are. ("Kick if your legs ache," said one of the Negative.) Then there must be another world 'cause here's a fellow scared halt to death with a mouse, and where is the mouse? Until my learned opponent answers this question, or shows up the mouse, it is useless to say more.

Negative.—My ingenious friend has asked some very puzzling questions, I admit. But they are all outside the province of physical science, which deals with the world we are in. Has anyone that left this ever come back to tell us of any other? Not one. The doors of our prison open only from within. Of what is outside these walls, whether a world of darkness or light; whether we go from this to a new life, to pain or death, none has ever come back to tell. In the absence of such knowledge how idle the dreams about a Father, Mother, or a big Brother. If we do our duty——

I.—'Taint no difference what they do, when the right misery comes they'll find out whether there's another world or not, and they wont before.

W.—That is all well enough for debate; but could a scientific fetus deny the existence of an outside world, the possibility of a future life, with all the proofs there are and they have of its existence?

S.—Most certainly not. No explanation of the facts of its existence could be made without it. Besides they have positive proofs in what they feel. And what is seeing and hearing but modes of feeling sensation.

W.—Exactly so. Now I propose to show you by positive proof from living witnesses that while we are in the womb of nature, waiting the birth we call death, we have just as positive proof of a world outside the visible that encloses us.

S.—I would like to know where you are to find it. All I have heard has been of faith, theories, and belief.

W.—I will show you a sect of several millions, who make it their life work to gain and testify to certain knowledge on this very subject. They are not taken into this, as in some sects, by birth or parentage. But only as they are able to declare from positive knowledge that they are born into an invisible world of spirit life. They are required to "meet once every week" to obtain, express and declare experience and positive knowledge in the invisible life.

S.—But just think what absurd, horrid doctrines they hold about the one hundred and forty billions of people who have lived———

W.—Hold, my friend. That is entirely irrelevant. A witness is called to testify of what he knows, not of his opinions. Suppose five millions of people in different parts of the world were to testify that on a certain day I had the toothache, I took vitalized air and though I knew all that was going on, I felt not the least pain when it was pulled out. The tooth coming out felt as good as ever it did before it ached. Could science confront this great cloud of witnesses and say there is no such thing as not feeling pain when a tooth is being pulled?

S.—Certainly not. But if they undertook to tell us about the everlasting condition of their neighbor's teeth——

W.—You would tell them you was through with them. Now do these persons testify that on a certain day they felt the pain of heart hunger. Friends who had tried it told them of a vitalized air found in the kingdom of heaven, a world of light, joy and peace. They breathed the air and felt for themselves what others had found before them. Not one of all this vast throng who fails to obtain this experience for any length of time but will testify that it is his own fault; he has failed to obey the law of the life of the spirit world.

I.—Fiddlesticks! The Methodists aint no better than anybody else. They like money just as well.

W.—That only proves that other people are as good as they are. These were not put upon the witness stand because they were better than others, but because they had made these experiments their life work, through many generations. Their testimony like the "marks" of fetal life is proof of a law that governs all. If the Catholic and the other Protestant churches required their members to give testimony on this point, it would swell the membership to hundreds of millions.

S.—Perhaps they only think they know these things.

W.—How do you know, that you know, the world goes around the sun?

I.—He don't know no such thing, cos 'taint so. The sun goes 'round the world, I always said it and I always shall. Aint I seen it, and watched it with my own eyes ever so many times.

P.—Now Science, since we make no such demand upon you as to believe in direct opposition to the testimony of your eyes and ears; but simply ask that you refrain from making these the only touch-stones of reality, will you enter with your friends into our temple and if at first you fail to see what Tennyson does in a man at prayer—"the God in man united with the God outside of man"—as drops of mingling water, be content to wait till you have thrown his light upon the humble petitioner?

S.—I will.

W.—We surely shall not be cramped for room here. For poetry is the science of the invisible world. Its subject is Man! The one word that answers all the riddles of the universe, as it did the riddle of the Greek Sphinx.

P.—Allow me to introduce to you Man—the blood of a God, running through the veins of an animal.

I.—Oh that's too horrid for anything.

P.—The great tragedy of human existence. A being with two natures, which combined produces a third. The trinity of Man; Body, Soul and Spirit, a truth at once too simple and too complex to admit of demonstration. The child's first experience of life is the bite of the watch dog, self-consciousness, which tells him that he has broken the law of God, nature, love, truth and goodness, to obey the animal law which is self. Self-preservation is the law of animal life, as self-giving is of the God life.

I.—If the fellow has sinned why don't you say so?

P.—Because my aged friend, you and others put such strange meanings in the word my meaning could hardly be expressed by it. We must try and coin a new word, which containing the active principles of this also gives the idea of simple immaturity, misfortune, also both knowledge and hatred of sin gained through it.

S.—Sickness is the word we use for violations of the law of the body. If you wish to say one has violated the law of an interior life, you call Soul, why not say he is sin-sick.

I.—But what if he aint sick on it, and don't even think he is sick at all?

S.—Are not your children sickest when they do not know anything about it, and dead when they can no longer feel pain?

I.—Oh, I see what you are arter. You are tryin' to git sinner away from me; and it is all the comfort I've got left, to say I'm a poor, miserable sinner.

P.—And you shall say it to the end of your existence. To make you perfectly safe I will draw a line between the two words thus, Ignorance—Sinner; and say as the priest at a marriage, "What God hath joined together let not man put assunder." Now will we put the word sister before sinner and call you Sis, for short.

Sis.—That is all right, I feel safe now.

S.—Don't you see my friends you are dealing in things of which Science can take no cognizance. People who deal in this sin business are frightened even to insanity, imbecility and all manner of wretchedness with the spector of a God.

W.—You spoke of children in uterine life affected the same way with war and murder, and even took cognizance of one frightened by a mouse. Now will you please answer the question of the worthy fetus of the affirmative and locate the mouse.

S.—It was in the frightened thought of the mother.

W.—How came it in the thought of the mother.

S.—She must have seen or heard it. (*aside*) How silly.

Phil.—Had there never been any mice in the universe could this have been possible?

S.—Certainly not.

Phil.—The mouse must first exist before he can scare women. Thought can not create something out of nothing. Where then is the God who doth so frighten or attract people? Some have conceived this world was created out of nothing by an Almighty Creator. But the creation of a spirit world out of nothing—such a world as men have always seen beyond or within the visible—no such miracle was ever thought of for the Almighty.

Sis.—It looks mighty like as man could make a better world for God than He could make for man. If man has made God out of nothing, He had to have dirt to make man with.

Phil.—Now Science, is this thing possible? Could God so exist in the world's thought except by having an objective existence?

S.—Science in no wise denies this existence, but sees no evidence of personality—a personal God.

Phil.—You see a personality of a certain kind in every atom of matter, in every plant and animal. Of all the billions of people this earth has fed no two are alike. Doth God lack that which the smallest have—personality. Hitherto hath man been studied as two simples. One given to physiology and law, the other to poetry and religion. Now that Science has entered this latter domain we propose to show you a science of Man; wherein the two natures are united, the animal and divine forming the human.

Sis.—Why don't you give us a man and not talk so much about one. Folks aint fed by talking about bread.

S.—That is the chief want. We would have a specimen, a living fact to examine, that we may study Man.

H.—I can give you one well worthy of study. But Poetry must first give us a picture of man's condition after our mother Earth had taken the fatal cup, and while her Lord was preparing for His coming.

P.—I see the animals that cover the sons of God constantly making war upon each other until the ground is drunk with brothers' blood. Midst all this tumult and strife nothing is so pathetic as the God in man seeking to find their Father and Mother; except it be the frantic efforts of the animal to get away from Him. One crying out in the anguish of soul hunger: "Oh, that I knew where I might find Him." The other in the terror of fright calling on the mountains to hide them from Him, finding no place to flee from Him. Through all this horror of darkness a strong, firm Hand is gently leading them, a loving Mother tenderly watching over them.

Sis.—I never knowed anything about God being Mother. I only heard of the Father, Son and Holy Ghost.

Phil.—Did you ever know a father and son without a mother?

Sis.—There couldn't be no such thing, cos where could the son come from?

P.—In the shadowy "Ghost" you have seen in the Trinity I desire to show you an all-loving Mother. My friend Science can see that as certainly as the two lines of a triangle determine the third, so certainly does the fact of a father and son determine the mother.

S.—It can't be otherwise.

Sis.—Well I'm real glad of that. I always did want a mother. Pears like a home aint full without one. But it seems to me I could know her better if I could see some woman as was like her, as Jesus was like His Father.

W.—That's what we are seeking in this parable.

P.—A poet of France (Gautier) saith: "Faith makes God, and love makes woman." Love finds a Mother in God.

S.—If this be so it has its counterpart or corollary in the life of the plant, which having its life from the sun constantly absorbs new life from it, virtually creating a living sun. In this way I can understand the meaning of God manifest in the flesh. The sun is manifest in the plant.

P.—A very hard, dry, disagreeable way to find such a sweet, beautiful, pleasing truth.

W.—It is well that Science should show us new ways of finding God, so that all that hath breath or life shall praise Him. What could we know of the sun's light except as we see it manifest in the useful and beautiful creations of nature. So we may know God's life in His children. Thus we have the living God, Christ in the heart.

S.—I can see that as we can only know the life of the sun in some living organism so it may be true we can only find the life of God in living men and women. Observe, my friends, I can not yet feel the same certainty about God that you do; but if your theory of the two natures be correct, man must be acted upon by two opposing attractions, the one of the earth, the other God. As like attracts like they would become animals were——

Sis.—Can't anybody see they are like animals, only a great deal worser. What hog is so bad as the man-hog in the gutter? What bear is like the man-bear tearin' folks to pieces 'bout his dinner? What snake is so mean as the woman-snake talkin' 'bout her neighbors? Tell about God in them, I'd like to see it.

W.—In the figure before us the Poet has shown us a Glorified Son in the form of these repulsive gutter objects. If this be a true picture it must be shown in life.

P.—That is what I will now do. Now, midst the fighting animals of the Asiatics were a few persons, who, when their temple was destroyed and they taken into captivity, took some of the altar fire with them concealed in their hearts. They preserved it with the greatest secrecy, taking their name from the diamonds on the breast plate of the High Priest, Essenes. Drawn by the attractions of the hidden life they "despised riches," overcame animal passion and sought personal purity as the highest good. They thus had the reward of the pure in heart, they saw God in everything. Then did one of their angels (messengers) assure one of the virgins; she should conceive and bear a son. So was the life principle conveyed from her betrothed husband (Joseph) by the law of attraction.

S.—A child conceived thus would of necessity be very different from ordinary persons; inasmuch as it is the sensuous exaltation caused by the union of the parties that produces so much of the animal life force of the fetus.

P.—This corresponds with what our friend History tells of this wondrous child: "No man ever spake as He spake."

Sis.—Why, that was Jesus and he didn't come that way but right from God without any father.

P.—Perhaps He came right from God through Joseph and Mary, as light comes from the sun through air. So His conception; with the supposed miracle of His mother's conception; was not the result of animal attraction but the attractions of the God natures, and it thus becomes the "Immaculate Conception" the Catholic church commemorates.

Sis.—I've been to that lots of times, but I never knew that was how it came before.

Phil.—This is not to be taken as the testimony of an eye-witness, but as the only truth large enough to cover the facts in the records of this Child's life. (See Mathew I.) It is said he was born of a virgin; his mother says of Joseph "thy father"—Son of Man—Joseph and Mary, Father and Mother in Heaven—Son of God.

S.—This fact, if fact it be, removes all the objections of science to the story of the Gospels.

Sis.—How are you going to account for the miracle of the loaves and fishes?

S.—By the miracle of the loaves and fishes itself. Before the boy had them in his basket they were in the sun's rays. By the slow process of growth they were combined through cosmic force in the earth and sea. By the more powerful cosmic force in the thought of Jesus and the multitude they were now combined by a different process.

W.—In the cosmic power of thought you seem to have a key to the mystery of miracles.

S.—It is no more impossible for science to see the electric power in thought collecting and centering around the walls of Jericho until they fell, than to see them thrown down by the cyclone. The marvel is that men could be found to walk around the walls while their brains were collecting the electricity.

Sis.—'Twant none of their business 'bout the 'lectricity. All they had to do was to mind what the Lord told them.

W.—Our sister speaks not unwisely. As thought is the power which generates the force it is necessary that the thought be held right in that focus. Doubt or disobedience would dissipate the force at once.

Sis.—Why can't you just as well say that nobody can do anything without faith—believing and doing what God says they must.

S.—As an expedient for giving temporary relief to the hungry people, the making of bread direct from the sun's rays by thought power, was all right. But it would be a poor financial venture for the people of this day. Inasmuch as the electricity developed in the brain is to be used as motor force it would be too expensive to have it pay. But in consequence of the rapid work of machinery driving men to the wall, it is time we began to experiment, as they are in France, using the sun's rays as motor force for machinery. The question of the daily bread is fast becoming one of prime importance.

Sis.—I'm sick to death of this everlasting talk about the body. Can't anybody see that the folks who has the most money are the most restless and don't know what to do with themselves or what's the matter. A child is crying with starvation and you give it a tin whistle.

S.—Perhaps it would stop if Sis would give it one of her tracts.

P.—Let me give you a parable of these things: Once when an eagle was hatching her first brood she heard strange sounds of little bills pecking at the shells and she said to the father: "What shall I do, the little darlings are unhappy, I am sure they are. Once they were so quiet, but now they rest neither night nor day."

"We must paint some pretty pictures on their shells and put some nice playthings around them," said the father.

"You just let them alone and you will see what their pecking means." said the old grandfather.

And sure enough the next morning there were the beautiful birds.

W.—An apt illustration of our time. Men feel the thrill and stirring of the divine life. The narrow confines of the past no longer satisfies the yearning. And so are men restless, dissatisfied and uneasy, as never before. We must give them better houses, with prettier pictures; five dollars per day instead of three, says one. They must have more books to read, says another. That wont do any good unless they are about religion, says a third. Books about religion wont do them any good unless they have strong laws; it is only the law that can help them, says a fourth. But those who have watched the way in which the divine life has manifested itself in the past, can with perfect confidence wait till the soul, like a young eagle, comes out of the shell of the past into the clear light of the present.

H.—It has been my business to watch this life in man for many centuries, and this is way it looks to me: The car of salvation has been slowly drawn along on the track of time trying to rescue a few souls from the wreck of this world. Now is heard the thunder and roar of an immense train on the same track, coming rail road speed. Some people are frightened thinking the old car is to be entirely smashed by the new engine and the train it is pulling along destroyed. But just at the time men are breathlessly awaiting the terrible collision, invisible hands are at work cupling the new engine to the glorious old car, and pushing it ahead with new speed, it takes all safely into the city of Faith, the New Jerusalem. The grand old car is religion, the new engine is science. While men thought one must destroy the other, or be itself destroyed, they find the one propelling the other along the King's highway of holiness, and drawing the whole world to glory.

S.—This is very encouraging. Still we must be expected to look after the bodies of men.

Sis.—Well if you can't do better than you did with Garfield you'd better let them alone.

W.—Well, Sis; what would you have done?

Sis.—I'd a told the truth the first thing. If I couldn't a told nothing about Garfield's body or Giteau's brain until arter they was dead, I wouldn't pretended to. I'd said: Now Lord, I don't know nothin' about that bullet, but you can see inside as easy as outside, and if you'll attend to what I can't do, I'll take him "back to Mentor." I would have taken as good care of him as ever I could, and I believe he'd a got well.

S.—I think he had the benefit of prayer, to a large degree.

Sis.—Praying! I should think so. One day I heard a fellow prayin' for him this way: "Oh, Lord; save Garfield's life, if you can. But if you can't do that, do something else that you can do. But what ever you do damn Giteau! Damn Giteau!!" Didn't I give him fits though?

P.—Why, Sis; perhaps he didn't know what he did.

Sis.—'Twas my business to let him know. And so I walloped him until he begged like a good fellow. But I wouldn't let him off until he'd say the prayer right after me.

P.—What was the prayer you taught him?

Sis.—"Oh, Lord; I don't know nothin' 'bout Giteau's brain. But you can see right into it, and if you see he's just like them men as murdered you on the cross, and you will forgive and save him. I'll help shut him up tight, in prison, while you do it, so he can't hurt anybody else; and I'll help you save him all I can. Pray do save him now!

S.—A more sensible way than the law showed.

P.—I am charmed to perceive our friends find such good in each other. And now that we are led to the Cross by the study of life——

S.—We are much more interested in the life and teachings of Jesus, then in his last moments, I think. Much of the teaching is perfectly plain to me. But all that which refers to a future life, after the death of this body, is like an unknown tongue to me.

W.—He never taught anything distinctly, except in parables, about the future life. In giving the law of this life, He showed the law of the future life; just as you in showing the formation of the crystal, teach the law and motion of the planets.

P.—I see this life as the fetal life of the soul. The first breath is a pain, the first birth throe of the soul. The last breath is the last pang that frees the soul from the womb of nature, and gives it new conditions to grow in the new life of the future. Like the fetus in its mother's womb, we live in this spirit world, and all our substance is drawn from it. We are, perhaps, more affected by it then will be possible at any other stage of our being, as you have shown is the case with unborn children. But now, while we are in the womb of nature, any description of that life, we shall be born into, would be as useless and mischievous as light and air to an unborn child.

W.—Men have made the same mistake in studying the words of Jesus and John, in the book of Revelations, as the pupil studying geography. He thinks the equator is a big band around the earth, the zones lines dividing the hot from the cold parts. Jesus drew men a chart of the invisible world. And His disciples, in all ages, have mistaken His words for real bands around the world. Thus, when He spake of the "leaven of doctrine," they thought He meant yeast; when He spake of Himself as the "living bread," they thought He wanted them to turn cannibals, and eat His flesh and drink His blood

S.—They don't seem to be far away from that now.

W.—The natural consequence of a soul in a body of flesh. But if they are so little able to understand the things of the present, in the soul life, what would be the consequence of telling them about the future? Mahomet undertook to tell some of these things, and he simply described an immense harem. Equally absurd is the heaven of some Christian writers. It is their own hopes and desires seen through a microscope. Wiser then these, the Great Teacher opens men's eyes to see the spirit world (the kingdom of Heaven) we now live in. Had a knowledge of what is to come after the death of the body been good for us, the time to have given it to His disciples would have been after the resurrection. But not one word is recorded on this subject. All is of the present life.

Sis.—Now I've got you. What about the parable of the rich man and Lazarus? Aint that Heaven and Hell?

W.—Exactly. A most striking picture of the hell into which sensuality and selfishness lead those who use their riches upon themselves. A most comforting view of the reward of suffering the loss of all outward things in behalf of the soul's life. It has, however, no more reference to the rewards and penalties of the future state, then the command "Thou shalt not kill," or "Blessed are the pure in heart, for they shall see God."

S.—Are the figures of "beasts" found in the Revelations of St. John then to be taken as the beasts in which you see the God—Man imprisoned here?

W.—As much as the lines of geometry of the bodies and objects they represent. They are no more photographs of our future animal world, than the stuffed monstrosities of the museum. The "lake of fire" is the sea of passion, the "undying worm" the inevitable consequence of wrong doing. Will our friend Science tell us what would be the consequence in his domain, of a pupil mistaking the lines or figures of things for the living realities they represent—the dotted marks of the map for a real rail road or real river, the little stars for the states' capital, the dots——

Sis.—Well! I don't care one single thing about it. The beasts John seen are good enough for me.

W.—Sis is hungry, and if we don't attend to the call of nature we shall soon feel the teeth of a hungry beast in our own stomachs, I fear.

Exit—All.

CANTO VI.

THE FIVE FRIENDS CONTINUED.

Enter—Poetry, Science, Wisdom, Sis and others.

Now did I, the poet, see the friends coming together looking refreshed and happy. Sis was like a baby after a bath. Science had grown to a fine looking youth, and was even ready for a little joke at the expense of Wisdom.

S.—Well, my friends; say what you will of modern progress, we have certainly found a pleasanter way to get an appetite than the wise Greeks and Romans used.

Sis—I should say as much. Why, I'd sooner hear the whole kit of ye talk an hour apiece, than to puke myself half to death, as the great Ceasar had to 'fore he could eat Cicero's dinners.

W.—Since we find the creative power of the sun's rays are sufficient to account for the varied phenomena of nature, the sun continually becoming incarnate in the life of the body; does it not, Science?

S.—That is the physical fact. Men are but living suns. When they die, or rather, as they die by the moment, they go back to original atoms, to form new combinations.

P.—Why, Science; that is just the way God becomes incarnate in man. Zoraster saw the sun as an image of God.

W.—But what I desire Science to do is to solve the mystery of the resurrection, and show us the law operated here. By the laws already known to you, are you able to account for it?

S.—Certainly; if your theory of a God be——

Sis—Now be a man Bob, Oh, excuse me; I meant Bub, to go with Sis. There's no "if" nor "an" 'bout it. If there aint no God, show us the mouse. If you can't do that, give in like a man, and say the truth.

W.—We all emphasise this demand. You have entered the temple of Poetry, the realm of the invisible, if you find it a real world with a living head, a first cause sufficient to account for all the phenomena of man's life and history, say so. That this Being transcends the power of description or demonstration, your disciple Kant has proven. Will you now accept this Being, as the first cause, or say as Sis does to your theory of the earth and sun, " 'taint so."

S.—Have we not shown a life principle in nature?

Phil.—That does not cover the case. Every atom is dependent upon other atoms. Where is the head or center?

S.—There is no way known to science to account for life's phenomena, except by the existence of an Almighty, Omnipresent Being. Therefore I will drop the objectionable "if" and say there is and must be a God, else there is no man.

W.—Well done. Now give us the solution of our problem.

Sis.—I guess he can, for he's fixed up that thing stronger than ever I had it. Who ever thought if there was no God there couldn't be any man. But how could a man know he was going to come out of a tomb the third day?

S.—Exactly as He knew all things. Being so pure the vital relations between Him and the All-Parent would show him the mind of God, where the future is as the past, just as we know an eclipse before as well as after the event.

P.—Tell us Science, can a mother suffer from the sickness or disease of an unborn child?

S.—Much more before than after birth.

P.—Then must God feel the pain of soul sickness.

Sis.—That's just what He did feel until it broke the heart of the blessed Christ, the Son so much like Him.

W.—We would fain contemplate the scene as the poet Gœthe, in awed silence. But my dear Science so have the children of men stumbled over this part of the gospel history, either thinking it an impossibility, thus invalidating the whole story, or else supposing it the result of some outside intervention unknown in any——

Sis—If you don't believe in miracles why don't you say so, and done with it, and not keep beatin' around the bush.

P.—We do believe in miracles under law. And you keep quiet while Science gives us the law.

S.—Life is by no means extinct in every part of the body the moment the breath leaves it. Many of the vital processes of growth continue long after, as is shown by the growth of hair and nails on corpses. One dying by the leasion of some organ might be restored after the leasion was repaired by the bioplasts, during a limited period. The long continued pressure upon the heart of Jesus, caused by extreme anguish, would no doubt force the blood through His heart into the pericardium, The stagnation thus caused would result in death. At this point the spear of the Roman soldier, by withdrawing the congealed fluid, would materially assist nature in the work of restoration.

P.—So doth God often work out his purposes of love and salvation for men through their own blindness.

Sis.—But where did the angels in white come from?

H.—Josephus tells of an order of Essene angels, who wore white to signify perfect purity.

Sis.—What about the raising of Lazarus?

P.—People greatly mistake, who suppose the soul (being or person) is born into the other life, as Minerva from the head of Jupiter, full grown and full armed. During its union with the body the soul sleeps, except when awakened by the body. Says Jesus: "Our friend Lazarus sleeps, I go to awaken him." Showing that until the soul hath other form, in which to manifest its life, it is latent in the body or brain, as is the life in the seed. St. Paul seems to see the body or brain as a seed from which the new spiritual body grows. This life principle is only set free by the decomposition of the old body. The brain is the evolved result of every impression, word, deed and thought of the whole life. Hence it is in this life we are, in a large measure, determining what the next shall be. The action of all vital force is due to electricity, is it not?

S.—That is the name we give to the active principle in the sun's rays. And if Jesus by the electric power of thought arrested the decomposition of the body, restoring the brain to its normal condition, Lazarus would soon "wake out of sleep." The restorative power of drugs is found in its greatest power in thought. To say one is cured by nothing but thought, is to say one had thirst quenched by nothing but water.

Sis.—What about the assension?

S.—The life principle causes the organization of the body. It is as easy to dissolve this by the action of thought, as by any other form of electricity. The fire which consumes and sends the body back to its original form or particles is only another illustration of this power.

Sis.—Well, I may as well own up to it. Since I've heard

so much 'bout natural law, I've been sort o' scattered in praying. Law is on my side, now.

Even as the friends were talking did I, the poet, hear the most delightful music in the distance.

CANTO VII.

SCIENCE REFUSES RELIGION.

Now I saw the beautiful Bride and her Lord approach the place where the friends were together. The Bride did throw a kiss to them, which each returned with the right hand. Now did the Bride and Son beckon them to follow, and share their work of glorifying Man.

At this point, I saw a noble woman of royal birth, one of the King's daughters, called Religion, come to them holding out her hand to Science, thus: She did lay the right hand over the wrist of the left. Thus reaching out both hands for him to grasp. Now Science did turn away and refuse to take the proffered hands. Grief did fill the hearts of the friends. And they said: "How shall we ever find the true road to progress, but through the union of these two?"

Then I saw that from the head of the Lord there went forth a life germ into the heart of the Bride. This did reach and vitalize a cell containing the seed of the woman. This new life, fruit not of the loins but of the head and heart, was now deposited in the life center of the brain of Science. And lo; as it sprang up it began to produce fruit, as the grafted fruit of the vine. From this life growth shall come the new wine of the kingdom of Man.

Now when they had begotten this new life into the heart of Science, I saw them withdraw and leave the friends to work out their own salvation, while they went to the city of Babylon.

There they did find the horrid Inferno, the Poet saw. There they did see the Hell St. John saw. Here was the lake of fire (alcohol), where men were daily consuming with the slow fire, tortured by undying thirst, vainly calling for a drop of water to cool their parched tongues. This lake of fire was transparent as clear glass. And I saw plunged therein those whose life blood was become as liquid fire, carrying death and torture to every part of the body. These did look with pleading, helpless, despairing eyes, but there was none to help or save. Writhing in torture with this seething mass of passion-cursed ones, were those whom the cankering lust of gold had eaten through and through, like an icicle honeycombed by the sun, like iron whose whole substance is turned to rust. Now were the demons Hate, Selfishness, Despair, Remorse, Lust, Appetite and Passion continually devising new means of torture for these unhappy wretches. Into this awful maelstrom of vice and wretchedness I saw the most beautiful women, the loveliest children, the bravest men, were all the time being drawn, to be thrown up at the change of the tide, the same disgusting, loathsome objects as the others. How I wept because there was none to deliver or save.

Now through all the streets of the wondrous city were men of all tribes, nations, people and tongues; come hither to trade in merchandise of gold, silver and precious things.

Now did this proud mistress of the seas lift up her head with glad exultation, that the sun never set on her dominions. And I saw that whereever her flag went she carried the "rights of men," gave to the world freedom and protection. But while she took light and bread to the distant

East and West, North and South, did her own people sit in darkness and soul hunger.

Then there arose a great cry through all the city, as each man felt his brothers pain though he knew not whence it came. Now were the people restless, unhappy, unsatisfied; seeking rest but finding none. Then did their mountains of gold become as volcanoes, to burn their flesh as with living fire.

Now as the voice of woe and lamentation did come up from the heart of this mighty city, the Son and His Bride came to the rescue. For she did show them her ring, which had upon it S. A. L. V. A. T. I. O. N. Thus it came to pass as the light of the Bride and her Lord was thrown upon this mighty city of darkness, there sprang up a knightly army, whose banners were SALVATION. Now these soldiers did wear the triple crown, the Bride did wear— Faith, Hope and Love. Soon did the glad shouts of "hallelujah" ring through all the world. The noise was as the music of all instruments in glad harmonious song. And the glorious flag of salvation did float on every breeze, o'er every land. So did this mighty army fight with the demons, did destroy man, did slay all they could reach.

Thus was the cry of woe changed to joy and glory, as the young men and maidens, old and young, childhood and white hair bear aloft the mighty ensign of the Cross, sounding the jubilee of redemption. So did Death and Hell give up their dead, and Light, Life and Love were in all the world.

Now it came to pass, as this glorious army did beckon to the friends to follow them, Poetry did want to go to the barracks with them. But when she did reach out her hand to the others, they spake thus:

W.—Nay, nay, my sister; let each do the work the

Divine Parent hath appointed us. They are valiant soldiers and while they do slay the internal foes of man, let us provide him the nutriment of eternal life. Those who have had the evil spirit cast out must be fed, nourished and led into all truth, else they will go back to the life of the senses; their last state being worse than the first. I pray you look to the promise of our Elder Brother.

P.—He doth declare the people shall not be left orphans (comfortless). But the Advocate, Comforter, Helper should come, who would lead them into all truth.

W.—So shall we be this circle or equator. Wisdom, Poetry and Science joined to Religion shall encircle the whole earth. Directly under the rays of the Son of Righteousness, these shall reflect His light o'er all the world—"guide into all truth."

P—A. C. H. E. shall we be called for short.

Sis.—You'd better call yourself the *Ache* conern; for you'll ache bad enough before you are through.

Law—Exactly so. No man can take on others pain without suffering. But this burden is much lighter when taken on voluntarily than when forced upon one from outside pressure. Saving through love is the lightness of the Cross.

Sis.—Well, what are you going to do with miracles?

Law—Miracle is only another name for the unknown law of certain phenomena. Supernaturalism and agnosticism are born of the same parents.

Sis.—Who cares anything about isms or flisms? I wish Poetry would jingle us some rhymes. Like the music of the merry chimes, chimes, chimes.

W.—All right Sis; let Law tell us the meaning of the wedding ring being pure gold, and then Poetry may read us that roll she fondles so lovingly.

Law—Gold is science, in the ring, holding all the diamonds in a circle. Gold is the one bond of union between all nations and people. Alike, an object of desire to the most cultivated as to the lowest savage. The latter is attracted by its shining beauty, even though he may have no idea of its purchasing power. This proves man esentially one, a unit. Many experiments were made before this one bond of union for all mankind was found, tested and proven. But inasmuch as it is proven that all men can unite on the platform of gold, it shows that there is no obstacle but can be overcome, to a union of all mankind on one platform. That no truth has been found in the past that could take the place of gold, in the social realm, has been the cause of the endless divisions among men. Each having a fragment of truth, supposing it the whole.

P.—Every idea, every theory is born of truth. Error, like darkness, is negative. It has no creative power.

Sis.—I should like to know where all the lies come from?

S.—Whereever there is life there is death. So, whereever there is truth there must be error or falsity; else truth could not obey the law of life. As truth lives it must all the time be mixed with death, falsity.

W.—Some minds, like Sis', are so formed as to see the false; others, like our friend Poetry, see only the truth.

Sis—You are tryin' to make out I'm like them things as feeds on carrion; are ye? Well, it is a shame the way you treat me.

W.—Can you now show us any truth which shall explain the phenomena of life and history, as the law of gravitation explains the phenomena of nature?

Law—Give me time and I will try, but let us have the rhymes now.

Sis—I should say so, I want to go to sleep.

CANTO VIII.

WOMAN OF THE WEST.

"And there appeared a great wonder in heaven; a woman clothed with the sun, and the moon under her feet, and upon her head a crown of twelve stars."—St. John.

Now time is born life doth begin;
Morning stars together sing
Glad anthems of creative love.
Earth, mirror, now for heaven above.
Ah! what a glorious dawn is this—
Thrills heaven with the sweetest bliss;
The rising sun comes greeting man—
     New form of God.
This bright, new earth; his fair inheritance,
All force in full submissiveness,
     Earth's royal Lord.
But brighter, rosier was the morn,
Brought the glad news " woman is born."
Oh! earth rejoice. Put on thy robes of beauty now;
Bring garlands fair to crown her brow.
This is earth's jubilee. Let roses bloom,
Fair lilies, violets, sweet pinks may come;
All nature with a smiling face,
Greet this fair one of wondrous grace.
Woman; the crowning work of God—
Bows her sweet face as greets her Lord.
And e'en as flowers blossomed fair,

Sweet-scented fragrance filled the air—
While heaven vieing with glad earth,
To crown the day of woman's birth,
Painted her skies in gorgeous hues,
Distilled her vapors into morning dews,
The morning sun makes jewels of, full soon,
Crowns dust with starry glory, till bright noon.
Now from the throats of myriad songsters burst
Wild chants of song, thrilling the earth—
Songs of such glad raptureness,
That earth had now such blessedness—
That all the stars began to sing again,
In sweeter, purer, happier strain
    Than sang at first.
And stars, and birds, and flowers all,
Come at the voice of love's first call.
Thus woman came, to rule by love,
As man by force his majesty doth prove.
His be the power, the strength of law,
She by the sweetest cords to draw
    All hearts to Him.
Like as the flowers the earth had decked,
Like as the clouds with golden azure flecked,
    Woman's beauty now did dim.
Life's golden goblet, held in her right hand;
Filled with the choicest vintage of the land.
Born now of this luxurious grace,
Come now to claim the first glad place,
Serpents of sense, subtle and wise,
Did entrance make in this new paradise,
The outer covering was so fair—
Joys of sense so thrilled the happy pair,
Saw in the earth such promise ripe,

Of immortal youth, and deathless life—
So clamorous were the senses for their food ;
All things God made did seem so good,
'Twould seem but right to pluck and eat,
What looked so fair, and pleased the taste.
Beware! beware! of sensuous cheats,
A still small voice now spake in haste—
Spake of a higher law, an unseen good.
That voice was low, but sense spake loud,
The warm blood flushing through their veins,
Gave no sure warn of coming pains.
Intoxicated with each new delight ;
Born of the day, what knew they of the night?
What marvel that the twain now ate,
Forbidden fruit, the tree of sense.
Intoxication's sweetest thought was this,
New knowledge increased life, fulness of bliss
But now 'twould seem at touch of sin,
A full armed giant sprang to life within;
Scorpions with ten thousand stings—
The fiery scourge that disobedience brings.
Writhing in pain with anguish tossed,
Moaning in grief, cried—*we are lost*.
The Father looked with pity on the child,
Heard the despairing cry so sad and wild.
Saw now the anguish of this dread tragedy,
In hapless struggle with life's mystery.
They shall be parents like as we, God spake,
The child shall full atonement make,
   For all this misery.
So was the Holy Babe now given,
To bridge the gulf 'twixt them and heaven,
   Bring new felicity.

With mother's love she clasped her boy,
Gave to the father's heart such joy;
    I've gotten a man—the Lord—
    Felt now the happiness of God.
As grew the boy, from day to day,
So light of heart, so glad and gay;
His brother saw with envy rife,
And now in anger took his life.
What anguish rent the mother's heart,
As thought from him she could not part.
Kneeling beside the lifeless clay,
Tried hard to waken all the day.
With fleetness of an angel's wings borne down,
A crowned woman to her come.
Daughter of earth why weepest thus,
Was not thy boy made of the dust?
Oh wake, my boy! the mother said.
Daughter of earth; thy boy is dead.
    Dead? what is that?
Death is the parent of new life,
Hushes the flesh's wearing strife.
    Free's the soul of God begot.
Fear not, thy boy still lives—
Whose death thy heart so deeply grieves.
With joy, the mother heard the speech,
Thought the new life within her reach;
And kept her watch beside the boy—
Waiting the coming of this promised joy—
    The higher life.
The dawn was on the Eastern hills,
A glorious hope the mother thrills—
    Sure, here was life.
With joy she clasped him to her breast,

Thinking the watch was over, she could rest,
That form decayed fell from her arms;
Shrieks out in terror's wild alarms.—
    The life, was but the crawling worm.
Was born in that dead form.
Oh! cursed promises she cried,
All of my hopes have so belied.
And black despair now seized her heart,
As from her boy she had to part.
Oh cruel, cruel woman; thus said she,
That could so mock a mother's misery,
With tears fill all the briny deep.
This the first fruit, the heritage of woe;
Earth's sons and daughters all must know.
Now was a council held above,
Each drawn by sympathetic love.
Hearts rent asunder by earth's pain;
God will repay by greater gain.
'Twas thus the dear All-Mother spake,
Only a hand of flesh can wake;
That dread death stupor of the soul,
The curtains of the grave aside to roll.
A brother and sister must be given,
To guide their feeble steps to heaven.

CANTO IX.

Hark! how the bells of Bethlehem ring—
Hark! how the angels chant and sing—
Unto you a Child is born, a Son is given—
Hope of dark earth, light of glad heaven.
The Gospel tells the story of this wondrous Child—
Tells of his Mother sweet, and mild—
Tells how he grew a noble boy;
How filled his parents hearts with joy.
And when a man he finally grew,
What glorious truths so rich and new;
He taught the world the right and true:
Pointed the path they should pursue,
'Twould lead them to the higher way—
      The King's highway.
Set up a kingdom on this earth,
Men come to, by a second birth.
Tells all the marvelous truths he taught,
Tells all the deeds of love he wrought.
How holy lived; how God-like died;
By blinded brethren crucified—
How rose the third day from the dead,
Who for mankind his blood had shed.
Who suffered in the sinner's stead,—
Now lives, Man's everlasting Head.
All power in heaven and earth is given,
To help men on the road to heaven.

Sis.—I don't see no sense to that. If it's what's in the Bible you are tryin' to tell, don't you think folks can read that better 'n the jingle of your rythms?

P.—Certainly. I only put in a few lines to call attention to the Gospel story. I think, as truly no man ever spake as this man spake, and lived, no man ever wrote as this man wrote.

Sis.—I never knowed he wrote anything, only in the sand one time.

P.—He wrote of the woman's sin in the sand. But as I read the story of his life, during the forty days after leaving the sepulchre, he spent much of his time in writing the original Gospel, from which the four Evangelists copied such portions as they desired. This is the mystery of the fifth Gospel from which so much has been quoted—possessed by the Ebbonite Christians.

Sis.—Well! well, I am glad if my blessed Jesus wrote this Himself. I never could see how such men as they could write such things as are in the Gospel.

W.—It would be still more remarkable, if one coming to teach such truths, and set up such a Kingdom as he came to establish on earth, should have left it to the memory of a few men, to put down from five to fifty years afterwards. Such a wise teacher as Jesus would know the consequence. Especially when the Jews were the only people of the world who fully appreciated the value of written records, and made a specialty of writing them. Surely would Jesus know his teachings were as important as those of Moses and others.

Sis.—Well, I'm tired to death with such stuff. Don't we all know the Bible is all right, no matter how it come? Can't you give us some verses about a baby?

P.—All right, Sis, I've got some lines here I hope will suit you. But you must keep still till I come to them.

CANTO X.

'T was in the year of fourteen hundred ninety-two
A far off world appeared in view —
A beautious land of colors bright,
Recieved her royal Lord at night —
    Land of the setting sun.
Now in this land Nature had made a cross,
And so Columbus did the ocean sail across,
This glorrous land to seek, and find —
Where homes could find for all mankind.
Oh 't was the fairest land lit by the sun —
    Land of perpetual youth.
Where death is made eternal growth,
Where life grows in eternal noon
    With freshest bloom.
'T was in this land was found the Bride
Worthy to sit her Lord beside,
Worthy to wear the triple-crown,
Worthy to sit on the white throne.

Sis.—That's nothin 'bout the baby, and I don't see no sense to it. What ye drivin' at?

S.—We must wait for the time of harvest to find the sense that is in the spear of grass; the active principle of the corn stalk. The Poet is but telling us the old story of creation, the fall and redemption, in a new way, and I find it of some interest. I would like our friend Wisdom to tell us something about that second birth the Poet speaks about.

W.—I trust you may prove a more apt scholar than Nicodemus. And at least you have a thorough knowledge of the first, or physical birth; which by virtue of the law of correspondence is the corrollary of the spiritual.

S.—There is this difference. In natural birth men are perfectly passive, and in the other I have been taught it was entirely an act of God, depending upon the faith or obedience, or both, of the subject.

W. Your teachers must have thought themselves wiser than the Great Teacher, for he said the subject knew no more of this than of the course of the wind.

S.—That might have been true of his times; but now that we are able to tell whence the wind cometh long before it comes, and which way it goes; why may we not be able to tell something of the birth of the spirits?

P.—We can. From the physical nature of the child is evolved the ovarian egg. From the Divine soul germ, the sperm or vitalizing power. When this invisible fetus, we call character, or experience, for want of a better word, reaches a certain stage of development, a spiritual birth is the result.— One is born again.

Sis.—I'd like to know then what makes such a difference in people. Some aint born ag'in till they are old and gray as rats, and some are born ag'in little children.

S.—The period of gestation thus varies in Nature.

Sis.—Well, I'd like to know how you are to get a man born ag'in, when his will is ag'in' it.

P.—Pray, let us discuss this question some other time. I am anxious to show my baby—

    Behold the darling child now given,
    To bridge the gulf 'twixt earth and heaven.
    Oh 'tis a sweet and beautious thing
    Has come such holy joy to bring;

(Eve said, I've gotten a man.—The Lord.)
Its pink cheeks like the dewy rose,
Distilled a sweeter fragrance far.
Marvel of marvels; little cameo nose.
Eyes fringed with down shone like the star
Which twinkles at us from afar.
Oft did those eyes sweet tears distill,
The mother's kiss with beauty 'd fill,
E'en as the clouds their tears dispose,
Of pearly drops form glad rainbows;
Had shining pearls in mouth concealed,
The sight of mother's breast revealed
              Its flesh so sweet —
Did tempt the taste like luscious peach,
Like apple blossoms come to greet—
Like snow drops come to earth to teach—
              Lessons of purity divine.
Rivaled the whiteness of the snow;
Rivaled the lily in its glow—
              When bathed in dew and sunshine.
New miracles were daily wrought;
As rising sun, each morning brought
New beauty to adorn the face—
New charms of wondrous baby grace.
Fresh every morning, every evening new;
Such was the way the baby grew—
Added new luster to the eyes,
E'en as the sun paints evening skies.
Painted anew the fair white skin;
That knew no blush of shame or sin—
Added new fragrance to the bloom,
E'en as the pink distills perfume—
Added new flesh to the round form;

All baby tricks learned to perform.
Dimpled the hands, dimpled the cheek—
Made rounded cushions, full and sleek
        Of the fat feet.
Pink toes outgrown their covering,
Made holes let in the air of evening.
        A cushioned seat,
Made of itself. Helpless through fat;
The useless legs kicked pit, pat, pat.
For something sweet it sucked its thumbs;
Used little toes for sugar plumbs—

Sis.—Well, that's enough of that young 'un.

P.—Why this is the greatest miracle of earth.

Sis.—'T aint no better 'n mine was, when babies.

W.—There is just where the miracle comes in. Every mother in the world has just such a baby.

Sis.—Well it's a pity they don't die while they'r like that.

P.—Men marveled at the beauteous girl,
Thought of her as a precious pearl.
A diamond of such lustre rare,
As none earth's children could compare.
Grew up a rosy, healthy child—
Of all earth's taint, pure, undefiled.
Lovely her face, as changing skies—
Fair rounded cheeks, and dazzling eyes.
Coral lips, could pout or smile,
Of faith so pure as knew no guile.
As light kisses dewdrops on the rose,
As living water ever flows—
So of her nature this sweet one
    Did good. To maidenhood now grown,
Had grown so wise in spirit love,
Shewed wisdom never known before.

Now on a bright and dazzling day—
The sun so long had been away,
And left the earth locked up by ice,
Held as in clutch of strongest vice;
The shivering victim of its Northern foe,
Now burst its bands, melted its snow,
Freed was its rippling brooks and rills;
Came sparkling down the sunlit hills.
The feathered tribes sang merrily—
Light hearts made sweetest melody.
When winter came these birds had flown,
In southern climes had found a home;
Land of the pine and orange trees—
Magnolias, dates, and tall palmettaes.
Thus singing birds and springing flowers,
Dancing streams made happy hours.
Hark!- other sounds borne on the breeze,
Glad laughter heard among the trees;
Tells how the lovely maidens come,
To greet the birds returning home.
To pluck the fresh returning flowers;
To dance away the happy hours.
And of May flowers to form a crown,
To adorn the brow of the fair one
     Chosen their Queen.
With stately step and shining face,
With queenly pride and charming grace,
Walked this sweet maiden to the pole;
Bared her fair brow to receive the crown,
     Did fitting seem.
Now all but she joined in the dance, .
This was to her life's golden chance;
With banner bright this sweet May Queen,

Stood by the ripling stream.
The gurgling waters kissed her feet,
The sunbeams kissed her face so sweet,
Illumed her flowery crown with light;
Lit up her face with smiles so bright,
Touched with its rays her banner bright
Of sacred signs, Red, Blue and White.
Now as she gazed in water's depths—
Looked upwards to the sunlit hights,
Came visions of the realms unseen.
Things dimly seen, as through a screen;
Saw Nature clothed in heavenly dress,
Felt love's unutterable caress.
Now o'er this brilliant picture fell
Dark shadows, of serpents of hell —
With slimy touch, and deadly fangs
Coiled around, and on each object hangs.
Now, as she looked through time far down,
To see the woman of the Triple-Crown,
So in plain sight, a serpent of this sunshine born
To coil around her feet, did come;
Shook, now with shudders of the coming woes,
Saw darker shadows o'er her throne.
With her flag-staff beat off the head,
Bruised now her aching heel.
Now clearer light dawned on her soul,
Prophetic visions thrilled the whole,
And in this vision clear beheld
A thorny crown, now 'fore her held
                By a Crowned Man,
In melting tones, who thus began:
"Oh maiden, dear, here comes thy Lord,
This thorny crown thy great reward.

With this *woo*, to my fond embrace,
Thy beauty, love, and youthful grace,
I pray thee take these plaited thorns
In place that crown of flowers.
This is the crown that I have worn ;
And she who is my chosen one,
Will gladly bear its stinging pain,
Counting all loss as sweetest gain."
Glistened the thorns in her left hand,
In right now held the flowery band.
Oh, precious wreath of youthful love,
The tones as charming as the cooing dove.
Long time she pondered on her choice ;
Marked well the clearly opposite course
     She must pursue—
As all the heavy crosses rose to view.
The laughing waters rippled on the hill,
Hushed was her breath, her heart stood still.
The happy birds' glad voices raise—
Nature's glad song—eternal praise ;
Chirping crickets, croaking frog,
Each feel youth's glad life-throb.
The happy dancers, gaily dressed,
As the bright flowers, robed in their best,
Marked the glad time with swift-winged feet,
Each moment with fresh joy to greet;
Nor little knew, nor little thought —
The fearful struggle in the heart,
     Their much loved Queen—
So bright and beauteous did seem
The dew, was on the shining world—
The dew, was on the fresh, sweet youth,
To sacrifice her youth, her heart

With all life's golden dreams to part.
Now, here, to pierce the bleeding brow—
With crown, the man of sorrows wore
Against this dread, and awful sacrifice,
Nature brake out in fearful cries.
Softly the night sank o'er the earth,
Gold light, mellowed in silvery birth;
Beamed from the o'er hanging moon—
Sweetly the martin sang his evening song.
Bright stars, bespangled azure skies;
Looked on the maid with loving eyes,
Whose life pulse throbs in sympathy,
With life's glad, joyous, symphony.
Oh life, how sacred is thy flame—
Life! Life! what joy to breathe thy name.
Can I give all this up? she cried;
Join hands with the Great Crucified,
Accept the dungeon and the cross—
And for this Man, count all things loss?
Now 'pon her, did her youthful lover look;
In manly chivalry, her hand now took.
Sweetly as birds chirp to their mate
Seemed come to save her, this dread fate.
     "Oh, beauteous Queen!
How thoughtless of our love, you seem—
So long has 't left our happy throng.
No joy in music or in song—
No sunlight in the summer sky,
Withered each joy, to droop and die—
When thy dear face no more do'th shine;
To thrill our youth, with joy divine.
Hushed, is the music, stilled the dance;

To give our Queen a fitting chance,
>Her royal scepter to resume.
Hope, fain would trust; will be full soon."
So soft the tone, so sweet the thrill—
Seemed to melt down the struggling will—
>Their hands did clasp—
Earth's music moved her soul.

Sis.—Of course she'd give in. No girl like that could take the cross. It's when the're sick, and the world has gone back on 'um, they're glad to go to Jesus. And I think it's a shame. I wish she'd a took him.

W.—I would like Science to tell us, what was the disobedience that the Poet tells us first brought this woe upon our first parents, and caused them to beget a murderer.

S.—It was the act of begetting their offspring by contact of flesh with flesh, as animals do, instead of spiritual union, such as that by which Jesus was begotten of Joseph and Mary. It was this, that gave the animal such dominion over the soul. Circumcision was given as a means of in part removing the curse until such time as one could be conceived in purity.

W.—Is it circumcision that has given such indestructible vitality to the Hebrew race?

S.—Undoubtedly. By removing an exciting cause of irritation leading to excess in generative organs,—a subject well worthy of study.

Sis.—I should say so. If there's anything can stop the badness in men, you'd better be 'sperimenting on that, than trying to breed maggots in a tight bottle. There's 'nough of them in the world, and the're easy enough got any whar. But whar's your men, as is men, not brutes?

W.—Don't be too hard on your friend. He has but lately come to realize the invisable world. And see how much we owe to him already in explaining things, once thought entirely supernatural. Is he not showing us that the action of God upon the soul causing its growth, is just as natural as the sun upon organic life? It was not for the sake of the *insects*, our friend tried the bottle experiment, but to find the truth of the origin of life.

Sis.—Oh yes, I know how that was. Maggots—there is no God. No maggots—there *may be a God*.

W.—No more of that, Sis; let the dead past bury the dead past. Ours in the present, and future.

Canto XI.

SATAN'S WOOING.

P.—Now strong of purpose, firm of will,
That made the beating heart stand still—
Drawn by a secret force, she could not tell
Whence came, whither, or how befell
Upon her brow the crown she bore;
Crown, that the man of sorrows wore.
The flow'ry crown trod in the dust,
While sorrow's spear her bosom thrust;
The sword that pierced her lover's heart,
As thought from her, he must now part—
     Pierced hers with keenest edge—
Of her true love, this the sure pledge.
All, on the sacrificial altar laid
Her *heart* the offering she made,
Down her fair cheek trickled the blood,
Now mingled with the crystal flood,
     While her heart bled,
For all the blood by brothers shed,
For all the anguish of mankind;
The bodies' throes, pains of the mind—
Of souls imprisoned in forms of clay,
Traveling in pain both night and day.
Angelic choirs sang anthems sweet—
Earth's fair deliverer to greet.

The new world sped its daily rounds,
Still cries of pain the whole earth sounds;
The ocean with unchanging tides,
Salt and sweet water in its bosom hides—
Gave back in vapors to the sun—
As from the birth of time had done.

Sis.—Now I want to know how the Poet can tell us that her flesh was transparent as clear water, on the 30th of May, 1880, when she seen this all.

W.—Only began to see it then. As one lands in New York only begins to see the New World. The body is three fourths water. What is there to hinder it being as transparent as water?

P.—Earth with unchanging phenomena,
With hateful, wearisome monotony —
Tearing down to build again,
In one perpetual round of pain.
Human hearts seemed born to bleed,
With none to care, or none to heed.
Human life to end in hopeless death,
Pain only yields to the last breath.
Hope, fuel for disappointments flame;
Joy, illusive shadow of oncoming pain;
Faith, shadowy vision none knew whence—
Receding from the touch of sense.
Love—despairing Mail of bitter loss,
Illusion, that at touch turns dross.
The bride, in orange bloom arrayed,
In widow's weeds so soon displayed,
Wither the flowers of friendship sweet,
No more the maid her lover comes to greet.
Wither the flowers of neighbor's trust,

Frost-bitten life trod in the dust.
Mankind, like gilded butterflies,
Dance one brief moment under summer skies;
Then like the moth licked by the flame,
Life's weary road trod round again.
Each new life as much deceived
As he who first this life received.
Snared by the sense deceptive cheats,
As foe, each man his brother treats.
To youth life is a gilded, shining throne,
Where reigns a king, the happy one.
Filled with delights, extatic joy;
Soon every bliss shews its alloy.
A slave the haughty monarch lives—
O'er blasted hopes forever grieves.
His throne to dust now turns again,
And all that's left are walls of pain;
A hapless prisoner now is bound,
Only to tread life's cheery round—
                    Nothing sure but pain and death.
Now all this sad, despairing wail,
Did this young maiden's heart assail.
So did the fierce, despairing cry,
Pierce one fond heart so near did lie—
                    The heart of man.
Thus did earth's great flood tide of woe,
Roll on, and overflow her so—
Her bosom alabaster white,
Now glowed with gleams of fiery light,
Stamped there a blood red cross—
Illumed and burned into her chest,
Showed earth's deep pain within her breast.
As dragged the time with heavy feet,

As rising sun new sorrows greet—
Weary the form could find no rest,
So near the heart of man was pressed.
In deepest meditation, anxious care,
Passed many years of earnest prayer.
Nor only could some gleams of light,
Light up her path of darkest night—
Cheer up her sad and wistful face;
Shew something of its former grace—
When some poor wanderer, hapless one,
Some child of sorrow, waited on
     In loving ministry of help.
Awe-stricken, wondering what could mean
That one so pure, so sad, should seem—
Whispered the story of the suffering one,
By earth's daughters and her sons.
And when she went her daily round,
Lifting each sufferer from the ground;
Pouring in wounds the oil of gladness,
In charity and helpfulness.
With bated breath the children cried,
An angel form they had espied.
So with her woes she gave earth cheer,
Who were to her fond heart so dear.
Such cheer can only smitten hearts,
Itself doth feel earth's bitter smarts,
Trembling beneath their heavy load,
Give men, help on the higher road.
Life stretched before a desert drear,
With nothing to give lasting cheer,
But burning sand for bleeding feet,
But, some new sorrow, hoped to meet.
Now as she trod this fearful road,

Seeking to find a way to God—
Some pasture green for fainting souls,
Where living founts earth's rocks o'erflows—
Seeking some bread for hungry men;
They would not hunger and thirst again.
Behind, her foot-tracks marked by blood,
Still keeping on this narrow road—
Heard now a voice, so low and sweet,
As in the dark the loved doth greet.
Come hither, dear, and rest with me
The glories of the Bulah land now see.
Quick, following where the beckoning voice,
Bade her to come, with sweet rejoice;
Her path now opened in a flowery knoll,
Love light did make the sun seem pale,
Refreshed with fruits of this good land,
Her unseen Lord took by the hand;
Showed her a likeness of the woman triple-crowned
Which in the crystal depths was found—
    Of the river of Life.
Now, as she stood in deep amaze,
Into the crystal depths did gaze—
Pondered with awe what it could mean,
This likeness of *herself* did seem.
Now when again the cross she took,
No more her feeble strength it shook.
Much easier was it now to bear,
Much lighter was her load of care.
The world seemed like a sunlit bower,
Sweet peace, its newly perfumed flower,
And in this vale, and at this fount,—
A table land on life's high mount.

Come now to her earth's sorrowing ones,
Fed by her hand, ceased now their groans.
Here mothers brought their charming babes;
Her hand upon each head was laid.
Now holding in the arms of love,
Brought to her unseen Lord.
Thither the deaf, the lame, the blind,
Were shown sure help and love to find,
    And all were blest—
Entered into the long sought rest.
Now wealth, come in a ceaseless flow;
All men did love and trust her so.
A costly, noble palace rose—
A mighty thing of beauty shows;
Adorned with jewels, precious, rare;
'Twas thus Sense would her soul ensnare.
'Twas like as though the god, this world,
This loving woman, would now woo—
Laid at her feet all his rich store,
That she might learn to love him more,
Than one had taken from her all—
Bade her, love death, to heed his call.
Satan, like a lordly knight;
Chivalric power, and kingly might.

Sis.—I don't see how 'tis you're alw'us putin' up the devil so nice. Just see how how he come to that woman, you call the Betrothed Bride.

W.—Call her Vesta—Purity.

Sis.—Well jist see how nice he was; jist like the fellow after this gal now!

W.—A very correct likeness. It is thus men are always tempted. If Satan, Prince of Sense, put on the hideous garb he is generally painted in, men, women and children would flee from him. He must cover his horns, and cloven foot, with garments of light and beauty, e're men can be deceived by him, and led to ruin.

P.—Thus Satan thought by every gift,
The burden from her heart to lift;
Tried all the arts of worldly lore,
To win her love; e'en as before
     To win her Lord.
Her honor, in the Old World grew.
Did sing her praise, same as the New.
Now did the angels anxious look,
To see if she her Lord forsook.
Or loved him less because of this,
He'd given her pain instead of bliss.

CANTO XII.

That serpent first to Eden came—
Serpent of sense called by what name—
So long had coiled round love's fair form,
Her beauty and her strength had shorn—
Poisoned the life founts at their source,
O'er earth's bright hopes spread blight and curse,
To accursed lust-bondage did give birth.
In this new land, the virgin earth,
The same vile passion did appear,
Had filled the earth with death and fear.
A beauteous maiden at the altar stood—
So pure and gentle, sweet and good,
And gave herself to one she loved,
Her maiden modesty and purity retained;
And when, by laws and customs long decreed,
She must give these to satisfy lust's greed,
Her woman nature rose in mighty power—
Her inmost heart cursed the sad hour
She'd given herself a lawful prey,
To the mad grip of passion's sway.
What was there in the words they'd said
Could sanctify lust, in the marriage bed?
In wild dismay her mother sought,
By direst shame and sorrow brought,
Together they might hope to flee
To the woman whom they now would see.
And hoped B. B. some help could give,
In love's pure rites they now might live.
Fair Vesta clothed in vesture bright—

Sis.—What has that woman, got fooled with that Elixir of Life, to do with this one?

W.—It is possible it is the same woman. Perhaps our friend Poetry likes to paint so well, she may be giving us two pictures instead of one.

P.—Softly the light illumed the palace walls,
As silvery curtains o'er them falls;
Mellowed by richest golden tints,
As shadows hither, thither, flits.
Around the sparkling fountain pools
Youth played on sand, age on camp stools—
Dug up the ground; splashed waters bright,
The Eagle o'er them sped his flight.
Sparkling their eyes, laughing each face,
Showed joy in its most sparkling grace;
With babies' winsome helplessness,
Fills every heart with blessedness.
Now B. B. sat and watched their play,
Each heart so happy, light and gay—
Mused how the little children come to bridge
Life's river, flows twixt earth and heaven.
Now on this bridge angels met men,
As on the plains of Bethlehem;
Angels drew nigh, and all unseen
Watched them as through a fleshy screen.
Hark! Hear those frightful, dreadful sounds,
The barking of the trained blood-hounds—
Borne on the scented ev'ning breeze,
Curdles the heart blood, seems to freeze.
With bark of dogs, sound human cries,
As man pursues his fleeing prize.
Panting for breath, and running wild,
The mother cries: "Oh, save my child!"

And woman felt, upon her breast
The burden of the maid was pressed.
Just now a man of frightful mien,
So cruel, harsh, and vile did seem;
In name the law of this new world,
                This maid demanded.
The woman clasped the trembling form,
Whose right to self the law had shorn.
E'en as a lamb by shearers cut, now dumb,
To her protecting arms had come.
B. B. now looked with wrath divine
Upon the wrong; but on the maid did shine
                With love and pity.
'Tis the law of God you trust, quoth he,
See, now, what God will do for thee.
The law of man gives her to me;
Defy the law before my eyes,
And as you take my lawful prize,
My lawful prisoner now I claim,
And bind *you* with this heavy chain.
Her beauteous robes were off her torn,
Dressed in the garb by felons worn—
Shaved her bright hair, the glory crown
Earth's lovely daughters do adorn;
And in the inner prison thrust,
Covered with filth and vilest dust.
Men vile, abandoned, cruel, mean;
Woman so wretched, all unclean.
" Where is thy Lord ? " they taunting cried,
" Pray, see now if he comes," thus they deride
Her faith; make mock of prayer,
When she their prison came to share.
Then was it that the prisoner rose,

Flashed now her eye, her countenance glows
                With love divine.
Our Father uses all these woes, and pains,
These outward ills, these prison chains,
That we through heaven's door may enter in ;
In purer lustre; free from sin.
'Tis not the outward claims, but those within
                  Doth hurt a child of God.
Let us now bow beneath the rod.
Full well, I know the reason why
God sent me here ; that I
                Might do some good.
I will enquire of him what I can do
For that flesh blinded man, and you ;
To lead you to the heavenly light
                  Where's no more night.
More to be pitied than his maid was he
Who wore the galling chains within ; while she
                  Was only bound outside,
Awe stricken in the presence such an one;
Now each withdrew, left her alone.
                Only in God could she confide,
These knew her not, neither could understand
Why 'twas she loved them so ; reached out her hand
To clasp the vilest of the vile.
But through the flesh, she saw the angels all the while
In loving ministry of helpfulness—
Seeking to turn each way to blessedness.
This prison stench would make the muck,
Enrich the soil for the soul's growth.
Since " sin cures sin " by God's decree,
I'll take the All-Mothers place said she ;
Give her my arms of flesh, my face,

>   To reflect her love, dispense her grace.
>   My bosom shall her cradle be,
>   Her children here may rest, and see
>   How she doth love;
>   Oh may I worthy prove.
>   This prison trust, so grand sublime,
>   Reflects a woman's love, so sweet, divine—

Sis.—Why, I should think she was just like that other woman, as made a bridge of herself 'cross the 'm passable gulf.

W.—That is what women are always doing, making of themselves bridges whereon men may cross from vileness to purity and goodness.

S.—Awful rotten bridges they often prove.

Sis.—Well the freight they have to carry over is an awful sight *rottener*, I should say.

S.—Pray, Law, inform us if what the Poet says about God's decree, that sin cures sin, is reality or poetic fiction, made to complete the sound.

L.—It is the grandest of all realities. That is what the letters on the serpent (S. S.) means. The serpent's bite contains the active principle of its own cure. The experience of sin causes men to hate it, because of the smart it brings to the soul. Whereas the attractions of God upon a soul increases as the square of the distance increases.

S.—Exactly the opposite of gravitation.

P.—This law is illustrated by the figures in the Prodigal Son. The father's heart went out with greatest force after the wanderer. So do sick children get most of the parents' attention. This woman ministry of Help, to her fellow prisoners, was the sure pledge, and proof of the invisible Helper, Saviour, Healer, Friend.

CANTO XIII.

Now on one holy Sabbath eve,
When those in the Christ-child believe
Did hear the music of the silvery bells,
The hour of evening worship now foretells—
Fill all the air with sweetest chimes
Worship divine, in music rhymes—
Soft breezes wafted to the prison cells,
Where men and women in dungeon dwells;
Fell on the ears of a repentant one;
Now mourned the evil she had done;
Waked memories of the bygone times;
When at the voice of these sweet chimes;
Walked with her mother to the church—
No sin, or evil did her soul besmirch.
These thrilling memories, brought the songs,
Of youth to mind. Rang through the prison—tones
Of sweetest song

          It was against the prison rules,
Had made it wrong.
Now as this strict forbidden sound
Did ring the walls the jail around—
Quick kindled was the jailor's wrath,
The singing woman was brought forth;
The prisoners' gag placed in her mouth,
Soon blood, and water issued forth,

          Stained her white breast;
Stifled her breath, could find no rest.

(85)

Mid jeers and scoffs the prisoners said
Try now your voice; raise now your head,
              Give us a song—
              'Twill not be wrong.
Arrayed in majesty, awful as—God,
When he doth lift the chastening rod;
Correct his children for their sin;
Through all the scenes this prison in,
The voice of Vesta thrilled the crowd
Spake in the tones of thunder loud—
              Release that girl!
And to the jailor sternly said
Daughter of God, is this poor maid.
Know'st thou; remember'st not—
What's done to her, by Christ is not forgot?
Trembling with sense of awful wrong,
Spake now the jailor to the throng.
With deep contrition, begged the woman's prayers,
That he forgiveness might now find,
Of the All Parent, stern, but kind.
So healed she thus, a sinful soul,
Hated his sin, was every whit made whole.
Now was a council held in hell,
Each spirit a story had to tell
              Of failure total and complete.
Meantime had come the god of war with martial tread,
With booming canon, fierce and dread—
Glittering sword and burnished steel;
Strode through the land with fiery heel.
Now men with fiery passions swayed,
Each 'gainst a brother was arrayed,
              As friends do mock each other—

So man his brother.
And o'er the plains the lurid flow,
Of burning towns through its red glow—
The war horse, trampled on the low and high,
Lit up with hate the lurid sky.
Flowed this strange fire a constant stream,
Cut down the noble and the mean ;
Till every house and every heart
Felt its own pain a deadly smart.
The god of justice now come to avenge
(In love) great wrongs, not in revenge.
Still in indignant, awful wrath,
Trod on whate'er was in his path ;
Alike the oppressor and his prey,
Nor minded aught either might say.
His course marked out by streams of blood,
Flowed through the land a purple flood.
Meanwhile in prison B. B. stayed,
So was the law's decrees delayed.
With prison chains goading her through,
With aching heart for all this woe,
Whose chorus reached the fleeting skies,
Raised now to God her tear-filled eyes.
Now on a night with sorrow fraught,
A messenger to her prison brought.
Oh! woman, can you hear this thing ;
The dreadful tidings that I bring ?
Victims of war and hateful lust,
Thy people, thy palace in the dust.
And where's the maiden now ? she cried.
Thank God, he said, that she hath died.
Then tell me, quick, what is the worst ?
I'll tell the story if I must,

Fair lady. But can never tell
The pain and misery has befell
Those come to thee for rescue sweet,
In helpful ministry you did greet
The flames enkindled by a lurid hate,
Licked up thy palace walls so great ;
With brazen throat swallowed the trees,
Fanned by the evening's stirring breeze.
Its fiery breath withered thy flowers,
With parched tongue blasted thy bowers.
A desert waste of burning sand,
Is all that's left of thy fair land.
There's not a man, bird, leaf or flower,
To tell thy glory, thy last power.
This only remnant have I brought,
And this through the wild flame I sought,
    A charred and blackened corpse.
Then did our lady raise her voice ;
Bade now her soul in God rejoice,
Even while the flames surged through her soul,
As fiery billows through one roll—
    Burns out the dross.
This was the soul's dire testing come
To try the metal, and make room
For an image more divine—
    Jesus could say, All mine.
With anguish wrenched her bleeding heart,
Feeling the sharpness of this painful smart ;
With tear-filled eyes raised up to heaven,
Prayed that her enemies be forgiven,
    " They know not what they do."
As thou hast taken all from me,
Now let me live alone for thee ;

As thou hast taken my loved ones—
Grant now this one request,
Love's strong behest. *Let me serve men.*
Joy! joy now rang througn all the heaven;
That thus to one in flesh was given
      Such wonderous grace.
Soul, body, spirit on the altar laid—
Holy, accepted offering was made.
Now from that prison dark did rise
Earth's sweetest insense to the skies;
Earth's sorrows knocked at heaven door—
Godly men heard, "*go, sin no more.*"
The Voice Divine—
      Spoke, " Thou art mine."
And now this light is given thee
To bear aloft, that men may see
Its sacred fire, reveals to earth
The holy flame of the family hearth.
Another name is given thee,
Vesta—Goddess of chastity;
The fount of life is given thee,
To keep from all pollution free;
      Let not impurity
Defile the life blood ere it goes
To generate new life. Life's pains and woes,
Its galling chains, grinding birth-throes
Are caused by sin, as Wisdom knows.

W.—This is true. But will the Poet tell us which diamond is meant here? Zoroaster taught of the sacred fire that burns on the family altar, while it was the Greeks who had their vestal Queens to guard the fire and preserve the purity of the Temple of worship.

P.—It is a blending of the two lights, as that union of color forms the purple. There is a great significance in the assertion of St. John that in the New Jerusalem there is no temple, signifying that the sanctity of the temple is now found in the temple of the holy spirit—the body. The sacred fire must now be carried in the heart. The mother must be the vestal Virgin, to watch and tend the flame that kindles new life.

This sacred flame shall be a pledge,
" Of that divinity doth hedge "—
                    The Mother 'round about ;
Father, Mother, Child in flesh—
Sure sign of that immutable reality,
Father, Mother, Child—God.

CANTO XIV.

Now, was another council held in hell,
Each with a story of defeat to tell;
Ambition, Vanity, Pride and Power,
Had each failed in the testing hour
To draw this woman from her Lord,
Who pain or woe did not regard.
Spoke now Mephisto, with his artful speech,
Listen, ye devils, while I teach
     The way to woman's heart;
'T will bring her from her Lord to part.
Go to the kingly sons of earth;
Seek one of Nature's royal birth—
     Let him her woo—
Strong as Greek god, gentle as love's sweet dove—
'Gainst such a man of flesh and blood;
What chance for her invisible Lord?
So shall we conquer by the sense—
     Victory, our glad recompense.
This woman had baffled all the rest;
Mephisto now took chance to test
     Her heart's devotion.
Now came there one of lordly mien;
Mighty to conquer love did seem,
     By law of gravitation.
Her prison door flew open wide,
Stood this grand man by Vesta's side;

And from a touch of his strong hand,
Chains snapped like brittle band.
    " Arise, fair Queen!
    So sad doth seem,
Come now with me, the fair earth greet—
Take life, light, liberty so sweet."
With manhood's arms, mighty and strong,
Lifted her worn and wasted form,
By prison fare reduced so low;
Through sharpest pain of earth's deep woe.
Now o'er her dress of prison stripe
Covered the flag red, blue and white.
Oh 'twas delight past all compare,
Once more to breathe delicious air—
Once more to greet the sun's clear light;
So long shut up in prison night.
Again to tread the fresh green ground,
To hear the music of nature's sound.
This was a noble, royal pair,
The woman lovely, sweet and fair—
His look so proud, lofty and grand;
Men to obey, he to command.
Manhood's power flashed from his eye,
Honor 'pon which man could rely.
And this sweet lady by his side
Seemed born to make a fitting bride
    For such an one.
His name, Alpasha; heir of an Eastern throne.
    Hushed was war's cry,
Lighted death's fires no more.
Stopped now the flow of human gore.
    No more men die
By brother's hand. Filled all the land,

With soldiers marching home.
Millions of bells with silvery tongue
Ring the glad news—
For all mankind, Gentile and Jews—
    The starry flag waves o'er the free;
With sacred signs, of colors three.
And on the land washed by the seas,
Kissed by the sunbeam's evening rays,
    Lives no more slaves.
This cry resounded through the world;
The starry flag again unfurled
Bore to sad hearts the joy, could save,
The weak; protect the brave.
    This goodly land—
Flowing with milk, and honey sweet;
Ope's wider her arms the poor to greet;
Offers her breasts to feed mankind,
A loving mother, stern but kind.
Now here a temple high was raised,
Where all men met, together praised;
Adorned with all earth's precious stones;
Filled with earth's golden stores.
In this temple, was an altar place;
The rising sun did turn its face
E'en as the Greeks and Romans build;
    In beauty all adorned.
Behind this altar Vesta stood—

Sis.—Oh, I knew she'd go with that fellow. I don't see what the Lord wanted to let all the devils go after her for; 'twas worse 'n Job.

 P.—Now when the sacred fire went out;
And darkness reigned the *home* throughout,
Love's flame, smothered in blackest hate,

Despair, a brooding demon sate,
Upon the family hearth—
                And hate and wrath,
Took place of peace, good will;
Each working other most of ill,
Then came the victim to this altar fire,
Whose holy flame was kept secure,
                By this sweet woman—
Would light again the holy flame;
To burn as in lover morn, the same.
Childhood, now felt the warm glad glow,
The happiness, did the home o'erflow.
Women's hearts gave thanks and sang,
Through home, the swelling chorus rang.
Husbands joyous now became,
Finding their lovely brides the same.
Now 'twas men's hearts beat high with trust;
Eden, would bloom as at the first.
No more would earth's sad bitter wail,
The ear of men and gods, assail.
Hushed into silence, be the cry of pain,
Earth's loss is now eternal gain.
Love, doth now all care beguile,
Tears, may now give place to smiles.
Vesta in robes of virgin white;
Sweet priestess of this holy light—
Spangled with stars of azure blue,
Girdle, golden fringed of scarlet hue.
Her face, showed heaven's peace, divine;
With mellowed light of love did shine—
Lit up a form in Beauty's mould,
Showed wisdom, half could not be told.
Now 'twas a helpless wife there came,

To tell the story of their shame;
How dark and wretched was their home,
The doves of love and trust had flown.
Now, as Vesta took the blackened torch,
And by the magic of her touch—
Now blazed anew the holy flame,
Should never let go out again.
     Hail, Blessed Virgin!
     Hail, Queen of Heaven!
Who to the earth such light hath given,
     Eternal love bring in.
As glowed her heart with grateful peace;
As happy was the lordly prince—
Come from the land of early dawn;
The land first greets the coming morn.
In his bright home beyond the sea
Had heard the story of the maiden; free
     Had choose the cross
That she might help the race.
Now, as he listened to the tale,
A purpose did his mind assail,
To look upon that woman's face
Had showed such power and wondrous grace,
     To suffer, and do the right.
So different this seemed to be
From all the Eastern maids, that he
Would fain sail for the West,
Obeying love's strong pure behest.
No shrine of worship had he found,
Had sailed the wide world all around—
In temples Hindoo, Christian, Pagan sought,
A woman worthy of his thought—
To whom he'd give the homage of his heart,

Who of his throne should share a part.
Through all the maidens of the East,
In all the beauties of the West
His Kingly father sought a bride,
Worthy to sit his son beside.
But his heart fountains were unsealed,
Its richest treasures all concealed—
Till that glad hour he saw the face,
The Woman of the West, whose grace
Was born of wisdom, love and truth,
Bloomed in a sweet perpetual youth.
This tale of love, so sweetly thrilled,
As joy and peace her heart now filled—
The dear old story ever new,
Refreshing as the morning dew.
      Nature seemed new created,
So was the womans heart elated,
The halo of this new inspiring glow
A wonderous light o'er all did throw—

Sis.—Well, I don't want to hear no more. I jist think it's a shame to treat a woman so. Now she's fell in love with that fellow; and how could she help it? And likely he's got a wife; may be a half a dozen.

P.—Now, as he pressed this sweetened cup
To her fair lips, she drank it up;
The sweetest thought it could distill
      Her loving heart did fill,
Was the great truth 'twas free for all,
Would listen to the heavenly call.
This thought exhaled a sweet perfume,
Like flowers in perpetual bloom.
Now sipping this sweet perfumed wine,
The lovers took no note of time;

Time glided on, as murmuring rill
The valley and the woodland fill;
With every morning's glad sunrise
Was some new beauty to surprise—
The mind from limitation free,
Takes all glad possibility,
And by faith's wondrous alchemy,
           Makes sweet reality.
One day came messengers from o'er the sea,
" Thy father's dead, we come for thee
           To take his crown."
Only if Vesta shares my throne,
Else will I all my power disown.
The Queen—may not duty call thee home,
How are thy father's people left?
Of all other hope bereft;
All's anarchy, confusion, strife,
Men seeking for each other's life—
Women westward look with anxious face;
Great Allah pray, send back his Grace.
Then I must go if this is true,
For ever since I have known you
           Woman and child are holy all.
So now I go at duty's call;
But thou, fair one, must be my bride,
Together life's happy stream we'll glide.
Ours be the wisdom of the turtle dove—
Whose cooing notes is thrilling love.
The woman's heart beat with new ecstacy,
Revealed in love's transparency.
Shewed spirits joy and sweet surprise,
Through the soul's windows—sparkling eyes.
Like sun behind a silvery sheen,

The heart's new life could now be seen.
He needed now no words to assure;
His love returned with interest sure.
Long they communed in spirit lore,
Feeling a joy unknown before.
Such joy flies from the touch of speech,
As spirit, from the touch of sense.
     Spake now the Prince;
'Tis now I seek love's recompense.
The token of two souls made one—
    Together come.
The woman turned her radiant face;
    The Prince with chivalric grace—
   Stooped to receive,
   The kiss she'd give.
'Twas the supreme moment of her life,
Devils now hoped would end the strife;
Angels looked with anxious fear;
If now the call, the higher love, she'd hear.
Lo! now as with supreme delight,
Looked to her lamp of holy light;
Saw there a danger signal given;
Her heart with sharpest pain, now riven.
What can this mean? in anguish cried;
    Hast ever had a Bride?
One but in name, great Allah knows.
Our fathers wrought in childhood, both our woes.
    A toy, a plaything!
Allah's laws, gives many wives to Prince, and King,
    Spake Vesta thus—
Go thou and wake her woman soul.
    Make her heart whole.
Now kindled was Alpasha's wrath;

And to the woman thus he saith—
>> Loves fiery billows o'er thee roll,
> Consume thy soul.

'Twas as Jove thundered in his might;
But could not drive this woman from the right.
Now did earth open wide, to swallow up;
>> All but her bitter cup.

All of her friends and worldly store;
A homeless wanderer, sick, heart sore.
Her legacy this lamp, and thorns to wear;
No more her head, but *heart* did tear.
Now as she wandered sick, heart sore,
Alpasha came to her once more.
This time in sorrow, sore, bowed low,
Showed how he suffered from the blow
>> She'd given him.

Spake thus: "You felt no sin,
But danger in the kiss I crave;
Think by destroying me yourself to save?"

Alas! how poor and weak a thing is woman's love. Writing on sand the next wave washes out:

"For you I'd brave the fires of hottest hell;
With not a thought what me befell.
But you, at the least danger signal given,
Would thrust your lover into hell, down from
>> The heights of heaven."

Now when she saw him thus oppressed;
Weary and heart sore without rest—
Her heart to the rescue quickly flew,
And though the danger well she knew—
Knew how the serpents lay coiled up,
Within the sweetened sparkling cup;
All these, and many more she'd brave,

In hopes the man she loved to save.
Now great rejoicing was in hell,
Hoping at last the woman 'd fell.
Mephisto, wiser, shook his head;
"Wait till you get her," thus he said.

CANTO XV.

S.—That woman you was reading about yesterday, my dear friend Poetry, was a fool. I have no patience with such trashy, silly beings. With such gifts as you describe, she should have made the world brighter and happier, instead of making of herself such an object as the Prince found her. Youth and beauty are the choicest flowers of earth; and for women to sacrifice these as they do to hide themselves in cloisters in modern times, or as the vestal virgins of ancient story, is a crime against humanity. As one who would destroy all the precious stones he could get hold of, or blight and wither all the flowers.

P.—Will our friend please tell us by what means this fair one could have preserved her youth and beauty?

S.—Why, of course, only for a limited period. She would have come to worms or fire at last.

W.—The difference, then, between this fair one and others is, that she sought to extract the sweetness of her youth; to form a new compound of perpetual youth and beauty, while they seek to preserve that which by a law of its nature is transient as the spring flowers. Beside, our friend is in too great haste to pronounce upon the case. Let one watch the fruit blossoms of spring. How soon they give place to a hard, crabbed, bitter, poisonous compound, known as green fruit. But wait till the autumn, and see how delightfully in the blushing peach, the luscious grape, doth Nature make amends for the sacrifice of the blossoms.

H.—Mahomet tried another plan to preserve the beauty and blessings of womanhood, and it proved like the wisdom of one who should pluck the peach blossom to save and utilize it. Look at Mahomedan women.

Sis.—Now there's jest no such thing as these verses tell on; women dressed in white, with girdles, and all this nonsense. Who ever seen any such thing?

H.—Julius Cæsar saw it to his sorrow when his conquering legions met the German Nerni, who were only temporarily overcome by his legions, but whose descendants overthrew the Roman Empire. So were the Priestesses of Oriental religions, as well as the Greek. Woman may be fruitful and multiply offspring by means of the head and heart as truly as the womb.

P.—This is the meaning of that germ of life that went forth from the bride and her lord. Begetting new types of humanity in germs already formed, including those who have thrown off the flesh, as well as those still in it, is a work the children of men may now begin. It shall not end with the life of flesh; but rather *begin*, as did the work of Jesus of Nazareth.

Sis.—Well, white dress, or no white dress, I'm sorry for that girl, and I hope the devil 'll let her alone now.

P.—Now was another furnace all prepared,
To test her love against her will arrayed;
Galling, the chains 'twas on her heart,
A keen and cutting, biting smart.
Like as a lion's power was prest,
Upon her smothered, beating chest.
But when sleep held in abeyance will,
The aching heart would joyous thrill—
Imagination find the god-like Prince,
Her heart, the will, would bid defiance.
Would live again the happy past,
The dream would make forever last.

Again love's sweet enchanting wand,
Would hold her in a loving hand,
Throw o'er her heart its magic spell,
As with the nobleman did dwell.
One morn, as waking from her dream—
So real, permanent did seem,
Came messengers from o'er the sea;
The King, love greetings now sends thee.
Begs the fair one forgive his last, hot ire,
Burned from a loving heart on fire.
     Thus the letter ran.
Since that dread moment I left thee,
No light or joy has come to me—
Darkness has reigned through all my soul,
Great Allah's power can not remove,
   . So I appeal to thee.
My former bride is dead, so I am free;
My mother's queenly robe and throne is thine,
If thou, my love, will now be mine.
Come to the golden East of rosy morn,
     Thy presence shall adorn.
Land of the palm and lotus, mine,
Pomegranates, figs, and dates, all thine.
Dost thou but bid me come to thee,
On wings of love I'll quickly flee.
Time and space be as were naught,
All pain and sorrow be forgot.
Then shall the golden East to silvery West,
Be linked by love's strong, firm behest.
On eastern throne of love and light,
Wave colors of red, blue and white.
The cross, with crescent linked, unfurled—
Go forth in power to bless the world.

Was this her bright and happy dream ;
More true than even then did seem.
Came back the radiance to her face ;
Came back the lightsome, winsome grace ;
Came back the glowing to her eyes,
With this sweet glad surprise.
As when one lights a temple light,
Makes all the objects glaring bright.
The cold steel thrusts her glowing heart,
As from these hopes she now must part.
Waves of anguish through her shook,
When to her holy light did look.
Saw there the danger signal given,
(Love is a law unto itself,)
Now raised her streaming eyes to heaven.
Ah! Father, cried, how is it thus—
Am I the sport o' malignant powers;
Amuse themselves in idle hours.
A foot-ball for the cunning gods.
Play they with hearts as men at chess ;
Their movements none can think or guess?
Oh this is cruel torture, double refined,
Torture of body, soul and mind.
With one wild burst of sad despair,
One wail of anguish rent the air ;
One desperate effort to break the snare,
With fleeing feet and flowing hair,
Now to the wilderness fled alone,
As once before sad earth had done.
Now heaven and hell entered the list,
To fight for the woman of the West—
                        As fought for the first Mother.
The woman with two natures on both sides,

Sense for hell, soul for heaven,
>> Thus did the other.
Waged now this conflict fierce and long,
Sensuous life was brave and strong—
Passion's fires burned clear and bright;
The flames came to a heat that's white;
But strong and Christ-like was the soul,
Deep its longing for the unknown goal—
>> Humanity so long had sought.
Deep was its love for all the race,
Caught in the snare of flesh and sense.
Thus even poised, neither would yield;
As neither army drives the other from the field,
>> Both slept in arms.
And wasted she from day to day;
So did this strife upon her weigh.
Now like disputes not settled by the sword,
>> Resorted to diplomacy.
Spake sense. What is thy recompense
For all this loss? *Cui boni*—this cross,
Thou whom Nature didst make a queen,
Hast made thyself so poor and mean—
>> For fools to mock.
Nature did form thee for companionship;
But thou hast made thyself outcast;
Thou hast a heart cast in love's mould,
Of intense life and passion sweet,
But when thy lover comes to greet,
>> Dost turn and scold.
Leaving safe paths by science marked,
Sights fully attested verities—
Hast followed phantoms, thine own brain;
Phosphorescence lurid bright,

Thou callest a *sacred light.*
Chasing fancy's will 'o the wisp,
     Art old before thy time,
    Such folly thine.
Are men happier for thy pain?
Of all thy loss whose is the gain?
Now listen to the voice of common sense,
Wisdom born of experience.
Now as sense spake so hard did try
To move her; a mocking bird flew nigh
To echo back these mocking facts,
To shew the folly of her acts.
Shrilly kept ringing in her ears—
Thy life's a failure, vain all thy tears!
Ha-ha! where is thy sacred light?
Where is thy Lord to lead the right?
Where all of his fair promises?
Fair to the sight, but fatal to the touch,
     Alpasha's thy deliverer.
Thus sang the mocking bird,
And thus it was she heard
Her silent thoughts, did grate her nerves,
Like saw-teeth grating through the bones.
Flew to the laughing stream,
     Where once a happy Queen
Had chose the Crowned Man.
Oh, what a picture did the rosy light
Paint in that crystal fount,
In place of the May Queen of youth.
Pale, haggard, blood-shot eyes, bent form;
So wasted now that youth was worn
To age. A frightful ghost
Of that fair maiden bright—

She fled in terror from the sight.
Alas! she could not flee from thought,
Who, like pursuing fiends, now sought
>To break her firm resolve.
Now like a panting doe at bay,
Turned round and faced her enemies.

S.—Well, now this is all well enough for those who like the jingle of words. But for a real true character, a woman worthy of the Divine Man, that one on the steps of the temple, sitting in darkness in the mid-day sunshine, while her love for the race wrung from her heart the cry, "if there is one lost it shall be me, for I will hold the last one before thee till fully saved," exceeds all others. These have but offered life; she offered her all.

Sis.—No body would do no such thing as that.

P.—Alas! how blind is both knowledge and ignorance to the glory of humanity. Did not Fletcher say, "if I may not glorify God in heaven I will in hell?" And did not those Calvanists whose ideas are so horrid to you, make the willingness to be eternally damned for God's glory a test of religious experience? Now did this woman only consent to eternal darkness that others might have the light and joy of heaven. A much easier thing than to suffer eternal torment *for the glory of the tormentor.*

W.—All this proves the wondrous power of love, which makes all things possible. Love and faith makes all that God doeth right. And though to the sense of others the thing may seem horrid, to the mind of the one who takes it in, it is the eternal right. Men may be never so much mistaken about what God doeth. But they feel independent of all evidence; he can't do wrong. And when men have the same faith and love for each other there will be an entire reversal of the false judgments of the flesh.

S.—It would be well if our venerable friend would give us some basis for such trust. It is quite opposed to all lessons of experience.

L.—It can not be otherwise, as you have demonstrated. One Force, manifest through all phenomena, so is there one Being manifest in all thought life. The Unity of Being is as essential to the life phenomena of the race as the Unity of Force to that of Nature. Now as this Being is One, it hath the same essential nature and qualities in the form of flesh as any other it may assume. The God in man is entitled to the same glory, love, trust and confidence as the God outside of man. If, therefore, God is Love, hence worthy of all love and trust, it follows as a moral necessity that man is love, hence worthy of all love and trust.

Sis.—I'd as soon trust a dog with my dinner.

W.—I suppose the Poet will allow us to discriminate between the two natures and only trust the God.

P.—Certainly. The most loving, devout, noble nature may be imprisoned in the nature of a dog, as Sis suggests; and though you trust the one implicitly, you must beware of the teeth of the other.

CANTO XVI.

P.—Now crucified this mighty love,
With all its throbbing bounding life—
A wondrous power of good did prove,
To such as warred the fleshly strife.
Daily grew a power so great,
Could help men through the narrow gate.
In loving ministry to such as need,
Helping all such with word and deed.
These many years had come and gone,
Watching and waiting for the spirit's morn;
Watching and waiting for her Lord,
His shining face so long withdrawn,
      Shut up to faith,
Which grows on promises denied.
Men marveled as her face they espied,
Women, at this unfathomable mystery,
Lay hid in her life's tragedy.
Once as in darkness long she sate,
On the cold ground thought the sad fate;
Mankind, victims of love and hate.
Oh! darksome thought to contemplate.
Remembered how men could be saved,
If their salvation, love, oft craved,
Would hold them to the heart of God,
Till the all-cleansing, pardoning blood,
Did purify each earth-born stain;
Make the soul pure and free again.

And in soul agony now cried—

To the Redeemer crucified: It shall be mine,

If there is a soul lost in all this universe.

W.—Well, Science, Poetry has been playing such havoc with time as you do with telephone and electric wire, giving us things before they happened.

P.—My world is not bound by any of the limitations of time and space. All is one, eternal—Now Here:

'Twas on one holy Sabbath morn,

She saw a noble, God-like form,

The Lord of Glory; (not by sight),

She knew him by the ineffable light—

        The God-revealing power.

It was a happy hour!

Oh! rapturous joy, how can I sing,

Such a divinely wondrous thing?

In speaking silence, hush my song,

        Silent be every tongue.

Parted the veil of flesh and sense,

        He led her hence,

Into the world of spirit life,

Beyond the reach of sense's strife.

This the new kingdom of the soul,

Healed be earth's wounds, men every whit made whole.

City of day, where is no night,

God's providence read by its light,

Shews now a shining, happy face.

        Oh! wondrous grace.

He led her to the mercy seat,

That the All-Parent her might greet.

Now did the God-head veil in form

Appear as Father, Mother, Son;

Spake to her now in spirit lore,

A language she had learned before:
Long have we watched thee, blessed child;
Thy patient faith, kind, sweet and mild.
Believing promise's proved false to sense,
    This now thy recompense.
Thou art a form of living flesh,
Reveals the Mother God to earth.
To thee revealed the law—man's unity,
With God, His true Divinity.
As Vesta mused upon this mystery,
Mahomet, with Arabian chivalry;
As like the Oriental chieftain grand,
Whose flag victorious waves through many a land;
As are the skies, the stars and flowers,
Reflected in the crystal bowers
    Like those on land.
    Thus spake Mahomet grand:
Most noble woman, pure and true,
How I rejoice to know that you
Have won the battle on earth I lost—
Won, though it's been at fearful cost.
For in the fight 'twixt soul and sense,
Conquered my heart by woman's charms.
And I did take me many wives,
And left false laws to others.
Ah! how I watched with anxious fear,
Lest thou had not the strength to tear
    The idol from thy heart,
    And from Alpasha part.
This thy reward for faithfulness,
For tested love proved truthfulness—
The Cresent that would never yield
To any army in the field,

Shall hence in loving worship bow
Unto the Cross, reigns supreme now.
May this sweet symbol of self-giving love,
Be honored on earth as 'tis above.
     Lord Buddha came.
On earth Sidartha was his name,
That brave prince gave up a throne;
Fled from his bride, his golden home—
Loved with the fondness of fresh youth;
A father's hope of child unborn,
That he perchance might find the truth,
Would save men from life's awful curse,
     Spake thus
All hail, fair Woman of the West;
Obeying love's sure, true behest,
     Has to a Buddha come.
Art welcome to their lofty throne,
To share the glory, all the holy ones—
     Their crowns by virtue won.
Go to the daughters of the East,
Shew them the wisdom of the West.
Now as he spake with kingly grace,
She gazed in rapture on that noble face,
     Had so helped the race.
A beggar child in fleshly form
Of misery and pain been born,
     Took hold her arm.
The spell was broke. Forms now fled
Like as thick veil fell o'er her head,
From that to this; earth's pain place, heaven's bliss,
This want and poverty. What change—
But in the child she saw revealed
Being Divine, by flesh concealed.

Its wretchedness come of neglect,
Took but a moment to reflect
'Pon the right course she should pursue,
Now gave the child the love 'twas due,
    Offspring of God.
Now greater than Lord Buddha came,
Jesus—the Son of Man;
Again the flesh was rent in twain,
    Forth glided they
To brighter light and clearer day,
    Spake now as spirits do.
His voice, like music, thrilled her so—
Waked echoes of immortal bliss,
Gave birth to peace none can express.
In silence stood before her Lord,
With crucifixion had her wooed,
    Veiled now his face,
Lest flesh should be dissolved. This holy place
    Was like the mount of Bethany.
Oh! let me look and die,
    Was the soul's earnest cry.
" Have thy choice, come now to me;
Thy robe and crown awaiteth thee.
The wedding feast is all prepared,
The wedding guests are ready made.
Or thou canst stay to flesh a prisoner,
With helping hand for man's necessities.
Canst take the light of this blest world;
Unseal the seven seals, now binds the word.
Throw kindling rays of light on earth,
Reveal to men their Divine Birth."
" Let thy dear face be veiled," she said—

Lest seeing thy glory, flesh dissolve and fade,
                 To vital air again.
And let these walls of pain
Stand firm. Can I shew earth the Mother God,
Unseal the fountains of thy word?"
                 The Master said,
"To thy true heart I give this key;
Unlocks the heart that you may see
The inmost nature; know when to approve, when to
    upbraid,
And when thou choosest thou shalt come
To this, your eternal spirit home."
And can I bring the world with me,
This joy to know, this glory see?
                 "All may come."
The condition's law. Who will obey
Can walk this glorious King's highway
In spirit, then, He took her out,
Above the earth to a high mount.
Looking down, saw men and women;
Like a dark phantom in bright heaven,
Now 'round the shadowy forms of flesh,
White-winged angels—ministers of grace.
But walls of flesh shut out the light,
O'er earth of sense was darkest night.
Oh! could they see what's all around,
Why keep they looking on the ground?
As she spake there came a youth
In fresh, bright manhood, love and truth.
Now as he walked with exultant tread,
Proud was his bearing, lofty head,
Came to a precipice, came to the brink,
Down flows a fiery stream of drink.

The sparkling glass pressed to his lips,
But e'en before the drink he sips—
A lovely seraph to him spake:
              " Oh youth, beware,
              A serpent's there,
Let not ensnare, for woman's sake."
The voice so faint; the youth but smiled, then drank.
Oh, Jesus save! Oh, save! the woman said.
E'en as she spake he plunged into the fatal tide,
Where untold millions thus have died.
How could you let him sink in hell? she said.
Now o'er this awful scene the curtain fell;
Another lifted on the spirit realm,
And there from out this fiery stream
Came spirits pure, and free from sin,
Clothed in white robes, all pure within.
It is enough, she said and wept, with hope.
              Again the curtain 'rose—
A lovely maiden, beauteous as the rose,
Sweet grace of innocence distilled;
With charming tenderness and trust was filled.
Followed the master of her heart,
Not life, or death or aught could part.
Ope'd now the grave where scarlet women lay;
Where hope ne'er casts a single ray
              Of light.
The woman sprang to save the girl
              From this dread night.
Now Jesus did new light unfurl;
              And to her great surprise
Saw such sweet lovely women rise,
              As Magdalene.
Now as soul's eyes ope'd wider still,

Saw temple on a higher hill—
The All Mother's holy shrine was this.
Oh music, help me sing the bliss.

Sis.—Well, we don't want ye to sing it, nor anybody else. Coz we know too much what mothers have to go through in life 'thout that.

Phil.—Perhaps the Poet might throw some new light upon it. The secrets of life have never yet been told, nor even understood.

S.—Well, that's not the way to tell them. If anything worth knowing is to be found out, it will not be learned by song, but patient research.

P.—Well, I have some very fine lines here that portray the hidden blessedness of the mother. But if the friends are so much more interested in the struggles and pains of woman than her joy and triumph, we can pass at once to the last act of the drama of this woman's life.

S.—It is not through the closing of life the race will be improved, but through the development of more perfect seed. Therefore, if there is anything in this mother's temple to throw any light on the proper genesis of man, we ought to seek it.

P.—I see a wedding party. Divine man and womanhood, like the waters of the Missouri and Mississippi, now unite, and are a complete creative unit. The man seeing himself a temple of the Christ, sees in the wife the holy of holies, never to be profaned by the touch of animal passion. The same law of creative love that first produced man now governs these persons. They would have offspring. Pure as God is pure, according to the command: be ye holy, for I the Lord thy God am holy, they approach the creative altar as the highest sacrament of life. The animal laid in sacrifice at the outer gate of the temple, only the seed of life is allowed to enter the holy place where God meets man in the sacred mystery of creation. The child thus conceived from pure seed, becomes itself a seed of higher, purer life for the race, and thus gradually but surely shall the black record " conceived in sin and born in iniquity " give place to the bright truth of the present era conceived in purity and born in holiness.

Sis.—Well, if there's any such record, I wish I could see it. Nothin' of that sort ever come to me, and I've been married long enough, goodness knows.

S.—Nor to anyone else now living. But in spite of the seeming absurdity, I see glimpses of a higher possibility of purer seed than we have yet known. It is probable that nine-tenths of the children born of distinct American parents are what in their language are called " mistakes," Science says, from seed entering the receptacle of the life germs through the vital endowments of its own being. We find the minutest life germs governed by the same law of creative energy; the same law of attraction and repulsion as governs the fully developed man and woman; the same law as draws the stamen and pistule of the flowers together. In fact, the same law as governs all but certain species of animal life. As long as the race is conceived by the animal law of copulation, it must of necessity be under the law of animal life, and largely governed by it.

W.—Perhaps the whole system of Mosaic sacrifice was but types of the great law of sacrificing the animal to the spiritual in our nature. But it is no use for us to think of settling this question without the aid of our friend Religion.

S.—Well, when she comes in I go out.

P.—We may as well drop the subject, then, till Religion can come in, because there is no force beside potent enough to control the fiery passion and bring man under the dominion of the higher law of his being. It is a great misfortune that our young friend is so prejudiced against Religion that there must be a perpetual divorce between them ; but I have glimpses of a happy wedding party where they are again made one.

S.—We never were one, and never will be. I have no quarrel with Religion, though she is always throwing stones at me.

P.—I see her in the not dim distant future throwing kisses instead.

S.—She will have to get the new nature she preaches so much about first.

W.—Nothing of the kind; all that is needed is to have each of your eyes opened so that you shall see each other as you are. But while waiting for you to make up good friends, all who are interested in this law of creative purity may have their doubt removed and their faith and hope in the higher law of conception increased by a careful study of the record of History.

H.—In every religion there is the same idea of a pure being able to reflect the light of God being conceived only in the womb of a virgin. It would be easy to write the history of the Virgin Mother and her Son, by collecting the histories of the different nations and tribes. I find it amounts to an instinct or an axiom that perfect purity of man and womanhood does not exist under the laws of animal life in the creative act. Pure as God is pure, holy as God is holy, does not accord with this act.

S.—Why, then, does Religion lend her sanction to it in the marriage state?

Sis.—Just because she don't know any better.

S.—Her bible tells her of something different. If I could believe that, as she pretends to do, I should have no trouble with this law. It says, Mary was a Virgin, and that Joseph was the father of her Son. Science sees no mystery here.

His.—But because they did not in the past know the laws of creative energy that govern the life germs, it was thought to be a miracle.

W.—But no miracle could make Jesus the Son of Man if he had no human father.

S.—That is so. Theology must either give up the claim that Jesus was the Son of Man, or else admit the truth of what his mother said: "Thy father and I have sought thee sorrowing."

His.—In looking over the record I have made, I see there is no difficulty with the gospel story now that Science has shown us this law. And in behalf of truth and purity, I think we should thank him for this important discovery—the law of virginal conception.

CANTO XVII.

P.—Hear now that awful prayer—
     Silence in heaven.
While angels in awed trembling stood
To hear the answer of her Lord.
This was the pain, had broke his heart,
And now she asked to share a part.
Herself a whole burnt offering gave,
For greater power the world to save.
Jesus beheld with pitying eye,
But could not her request deny.
It is her right, he justly spake,
Atonement for earth's sins to make.
The All Mother's heart's pierced by the cry
Of mothers weeping as their children die.
The joys and victories of her latter days
Had been as one aside now lays,
     Strength for oncoming pain.
So to prepare for this dread hour,
     When hell should try again
To break the chain of heaven's power.
And she who had so loved all men;
Whose heart a looking glass had been;
Drew out the good as magnet draws the steel,
To make men see, cause them to feel
     The God within—
Was now to feel the utmost power of hate,
Called to contend with that dread fate,
     Binds man to sin.

Bands only death of self can rend,
The soul, a conquerer, upward send.
Darkness now gathered round her soul;
Could hear hell's threatening thunders roll;
Flashed lurid lightnings from afar—
Revealed the senses, endless war
                    On soul and God.
And as she looked with trembling fear,
Dreading each moment she should hear,
                    (Or fall the uplifted sword),
The awful words, depart ye cursed,
Into the fire where burns the worst.
History, its dark pages did unroll;
Told of the victory of sense o'er soul.
Read on each page by lurid light,
How had the wrong o'ercome the right—
How were God's children crucified;
Nature and heaven, in anguish cried,
In bitter travail of soul birth—
The crowning torture of this earth.
As gazed in horror on this awful scene;
Began a movement of the screen,
That had the worst concealed.
Now before her was revealed
Brothers she loved, dripping with blood;
Filled with satanic hate now stood.
Frozen with horror, she beheld
All hopeful trusts were here dispelled.
The God in man hides now his face,
Could only see a sin-cursed race,
Prey of the worm that never dies—
The gnawing pain from expression flies;
Only by silence can be told,

Like to that force the whirlwind holds
    Itself in stillness.
Thus did the force of this dread agony hold silence,
Lit by this lurid glare of hate,
Earth's children, silent spectres, sate;
Like ghostly phantoms of a dream,
Upon the banks of the crimson stream—
Started in Eden through earth flows;
While from the hells came lurid glows
Of fires of passion, has its birth—
    (God pity earth),
In every seed from which man springs.
Earth and hell the chorus rings—
    Lascivious songs,
    In every tongue,
Tells victory of lust o'er love.
This crimson stream started from Abel's veins,
As flows through earth into its bosom drains;
The holiest, purest blood of every name.
While tortured earth, as if to shame
The folly of a brother's hate—
Hides from the wondering skies her pain,
On these hellfires sends the sweet rain—
Makes flowers bloom on battle fields,
A richer, sweeter, harvest yields.
In one wild rush of blank despair,
The blood in Vesta's heart leaped to her head,
Prostrate now fell as one that's dead.
Frozen with horror, pale and cold;
Killed by an anguish can't be told.
'Twas now the angels looked to see
Jesus would do in this extremity.
Her heart is crushed by sight of blood,

SATAN'S WOOING.

Been shed by hate. The remedy shall be—
    That shed by me.
Bade one take to her lips the holy wine;
Said he shews forth the blood of mine,
    Shed for the race.
  Thus the atoneing grace,
Warm and fresh from the brother's heart
Had from his own taken a part,
    Its life-renewing power—
    In this glad hour.
Brought back life currents to their place,
Gave back the woman to the race.
Though baffled, Satan will not yield,
While sense and passion are in the field.
The woman further must be tried,
To see if aught could turn aside,
Swerve hair-breadth from the path of right.
Rallied all senses, cunning might.
Hell's forces stood in dread array,
To ope the conflict on the coming day.
Lo! in the night a council meets;
Each with defeat the other greets.
So hell's plans are now all changed,
In other order now arranged.
Meanwhile in dreams and visions sweet,
Vesta saw all at her Lord's feet;
Restored to self, in gratitude and praise,
Chanted and sang glad, happy lays.
Or, cradled on the All Mother's breast,
Rejoicing in the long sought rest—
As troubled children, lost and found;
When once again they hear the sound,
The mother's voice. And all rejoice.
    List, now she hears

Sweet murmuring music from afar,
Late land of conflict and of war.
This not the sound of joy that gains
A victory, the price of brother's pains.
This was the music brother's joy distills,
When peace another heart now thrills.
All tremulous with joy, near and more near;
The voices comes till in her ear,
Soothing, caressing, fond and dear—
                    Distinct could hear,
The war is over. Take your rest,
As is your right; who have so blest
                    Our Father's children.
Such victory only woman's love could win;
O'er the dark realms of sense and sin.
Rest from your toil, with Christ enjoy
The gladness of the whole world's joy.
As echo through the forest softly roll,
This warbling music through the soul—
Sense held in this delicious calm,
Appears the outlines of a shadowy form;
Grows more distinct to enraptured sight,
Shines with a beauteous radiant light,
Halo of glory crowned his head,
While in each hand, so tenderly now led;
Cherubic vision of sweet youth.
Oh, lady fair, behold the truth,
                    You sought so earnestly.
This man a hero-god now seemed;
Enveloped in a veil that screened
                    From curiosity.
Saw now the likeness of her lawyer friend,
                    Brutus his name.

In love's solicitude did o'er her bend,
                Lit up new flame.
As now before her with him stood,
A wicked, unkempt, strange-looking brood
Of children; gathered from the street
Of the great city, come to greet
The one had found the Mother God.
How little did these children seem
Like the sweet cherubs of her dream.
Sought of her Lord to know the mystery,
These were the spiritual bodies you did see,
                Shews the glad possibility
Is hidden from the outward sight;
Seen only by thy faith's clear light.
                Then was she glad,
Gave them a mother's care, as though each had
                Been born of her.
Thus works
Kept time and step with faith.
While waves of happiness come and go,
Like dazzling pictures of a show,
Where each is thought to be the best;
Till artist finger paints the rest.
Fleshly walls no more a prison seemed;
Only a veil the spirit screened.
Thus was the New Jerusalem come down,
                Glad earth to crown.
Living a new life for the race,
Came back the brightness to her face—
Came back the glowing to her eyes;
Was to mankind a glad surprise.
Being of strength and righteousness,
Diffusing joy and brightness,
Speaking with power. Oh, happy hour.

Sis.—I thought you was to tell us of something awful bad. I am sure that's nothin'.

P.—Well, I have a few pages here that describe the joy and victory of overcoming self, but I can skip them.

CANTO XVIII.

Now 'twas the time had fully come;
(All other work was now well done),
For answering of Vesta's prayer.
Now Jesus did the furnace all prepare,
But when 'twas ready for her heart
From her, it seemed, he could not part.
Fain would he to her rescue come,
And ne'er again leave her alone.
Felt now as o'er Jerusalem he wept,
While on volcanic fires the people slept.
Fain would he reach out arms of love,
Take her at once to home above.
     But he had promised,
And she had trusted to his word,
In all things to be like her Lord.
No! He must leave her now alone,
Until her work was fully done.
Farewell, dear one, I'll come again,
With me you shall forever reign.
Came now a servant to our lady dear,
A maiden is awaiting here.
Seeing upon her form the scarlet brand,
When no wedding ring 's upon the hand;
I bade be gone, nor seek to stain
This temple with her touch of shame,
     Whereat she fell upon the steps.
Then kindled was the woman's wrath;
Followed the servant down the path,

Where, on the steps, the outer gate,
A wretched maiden upright sate,
As though struck by a thunder-bolt;
Her life had spent, her breath had choked.
Ah! she was beautiful and fair—
Such silky tresses of golden hair;
On which the rosy sunlight fell,
And on her face sad tale did tell.
With all a mother's tender love,
Vesta, with all her skill now strove;
Bring back the life it seemed had fled,
     So like the dead,
In all her girlish beauty lay—
So like a lost child sat down to pray.
Nature, with cunning workmanship,
Formed this dear maiden for companionship.
Could no more stand alone than tender vine
Seeks for the oak, its arms to entwine.
Now with signs of returning life,
Came that dread agony of mortal strife,
When woman goes into the jaws of death;
To give another being breath.
The great dread mystery of man's birth;
The awful tragedy of this earth.
When Zion travails 'twas foretold
By the prophetic seers of old,
She should have victory o'er her foes.
So to the All-Parent Vesta brought the woes
Of this poor suffering child of pain,
Asked for her life in the Son's name.
Now felt such joy her prayer was heard;
While yearning love her bosom stirred.
Now coming to the watchers spake:

Rejoice, now, for the maiden's sake,
                     For she shall live.
My Lord did now this assurance give,
Now came the last and final strife,
That e'en as Rachel's, cost a life.
Though not like her's, for this one gave
Her life for death; for naught could save,
Such was the power of poison took,
When felt of God, and man forsook.
When Vesta saw that life was fled,
No doubt could be the maid was dead.
Those trusted promises had failed;
Hell's force combined her soul assailed.
Despair, like lion, seized her heart,
Tore quivering nerves, tore flesh apart.
With one long-drawn, despairing cry,
Laid in the dust and begged to die.
What time laid thus, she never knew;
Nor to the mystery saw any clew.
While she, contending with the hosts of hell,
Upon a pilgrim's wife the burden fell,
Preparing the corpse for burial.
Who, in heathen ignorance of the crime,
This maiden's life the forfeit paid,
In beauteous garb with pearls did shine;
In virgin white the lovely form arrayed.
Helped by a serving woman kind—
Death, common bond, of all mankind.
Princess and peasant together wrought,
Each one's religious rite now brought.
The Crescent and the Cross, in harmony,
Now worked together lovingly.
The fight began in Abraham's tent,

When Hagar to the wilderness was sent,
Was hushed in silence, o'er this clay.
Some promise of a coming day,
When woman's love should still earth's strife,
And death, be swallowed up in life.
Meanwhile a man stole in the room ;
Enveloped in the deepest gloom.
A noble man of generous look,
Seemed now of hope and faith, forsook.
As wrought these women at their task,
Made of the window shades a mask,
      His form to conceal.
But when they brought the lovely child,
Haggard his look, frantic and wild,
He took a powder from his vest,
Trembling his limbs, heaving his chest—
Took now this portion, sure to end
His life; soul, to eternity send.
" Faith, now 'tis like the holy child ;"
Spake now the serving woman mild.
" And she the Blessed Virgin bless."
Thus they the lovely babe did dress ;
And laid it on its mother's breast ;
In hopes of an eternal rest.
" Sure, some one's stole her wedding ring,"
The weeping woman fondly said,
As her own crucifix she'd bring,
And on her bosom fondly laid.
Sure, this must blot out all the stain,
If any such should still remain.
Sprinkled with holy water, what was left ;
When body of the soul's bereft.
     Alone with the dead.

Upon the corpse, the stranger laid his head.
Took from his vest a paper roll,
Wrote out a little scrawl.
And when the serving maid returned,
To trim the candles as they burned
Beside the babe; now lifeless clay—
                    The father lay.
The woman took the paper from his hand,
Its meaning could not understand.
Vesta was now aroused as from a dream,
So strange, bewildering did seem,
And on her shoulder a policeman laid
His hand. I take you prisoner, he said.
This was the sight that Vesta saw,
Dragged by the officer of the law
To where death's victims now were lain;
Each had by poison, here been slain.
                    The officer now spoke—
What means this murder here revealed,
You have tried so hard to keep concealed.
                    Answer for justice sake.
Let this triple murder be explained.
Stupid with wonder, she exclaimed—
                    I know no more than you.
The officer said, this can't be true.
As on these victims she did look,
Her frame with mortal anguish shook,
To see this father, mother, child.
And with low, cry, despairing wild—
As the truth upon her mind did flash;
Fell to the earth, in helpless crash.
When reason 'gain come to its throne,
She was in prison all alone.

Darkness reigned without; within,
Alone, she struggled with the hosts of sin.
Her former friends now her denied;
Cried, as of old: Let her be crucified.
Now, when before the judge was brought,
     She trusting thought—
Surely her former lawyer friend,
     Would her defend.
But when the indictment was now brought
It was the work that Brutus wrought.
With a low cry of pain; now fell
To earth. Her soul in hell.
And what she saw, what there befell;
Her palsied tongue refused to tell.
Such horror, can no more fit speech,
Than mortals to the skies can reach.
When back to sense's realm she came.
Of her friend Brutus, they told great shame.
And brought a paper she should sign,
'Twould prove him guilty of a crime.
When Vesta had the paper read;
To his accusers, thus she said—
The truth is not, as this doth seem.
He is not base, cruel, and mean.
And sure his friends should not assail
The faults, he doth truly bewail.
     Spake the witnesses—
See how he tries to ruin you,
Like as a blood-hound doth pursue
     You, to your death.
It must be, that he thinks it duty sure.
For he is god-like, noble, pure.
Sooner than blot, on his fair name,

I'll suffer this eternal shame.
Saying which, the paper in her hand she took,
While sad, but strongest purpose shook,
With manacled hands, tore it in shreds—
As one, who some discovery dreads.
Though Brutus slay me, yet will I trust in him.
" *Gone, stark mad* "—they left her to her fate;
Felt all their help was now too late.
Now, when unto the courtroom brought,
'Twas only of the Lord she thought.
These men were instruments of his will;
In all her pain she trusted still,
When her accusers waxed so eloquent
Brought forth, the facts did seem so potent
To prove abortion, and murder too—
Declared that hanging was her due;
It was no more to her than 'twere to souls,
In Dante's dread Inferno rolls.
What other torture could there be
For one forsook by such as He,
    The Lord she loved?
Now 'twas that Brutus' wrath waxed hot,
His former friendship was forgot;
The secret learned when was her friend
With all the other proofs did blend —
    Cried out vehemently,
In that vile den, called holy shrine,
Lured pilgrims from every land and clime;
This *sorceress*, falsely called Queen,
Angel of light did surely seem;
Using her arts to destroy the young,
Sent to the grave, unwept, unsung.
But justice now has found her out,

Guilty she is without a doubt.
"Prisoner, stand up," the judge now spake,
"Have you any plea to make?
What say you to the sentence of the law?"
Strained now her eyes, as though the invisable saw.
She could not rise, but upright sate,
No word to save her from this fate;
Good Friday execution day was set.
All mocked; only the scarlet women met,
                To weep for her.
Meanwhile hell other council called,
While angels still looked on, appalled—
Marveling always what this could mean,
So cruel of her Lord, did seem.
Spake Beelzebub, arch-fiend of sense
(Mephisto showed mock reverence),
This is not one through heart, to win
Into the luring bait of sin.
'Tis through conscience must be won
Her present loves, here to disown.
There is a holy father on our ground:
Some way to blind him must be found.

Alone in darkest cell sweet Vesta sate,
Nor had she slept, though 'twas so late.
The sound of hammer told her fate,
Struck her nerves as torture dire,
Flowed now her blood as frozen fire
                Through all her veins—
None to regard or soothe her pains.
Waiting in pain lay on the floor.
As opened now the prison door;

A welcome light in this dark place,
Showed now the holy father's face.
With joy, as one a lover greets,
Did she her old confessor meet,
			Spake thus:
" The holy church sends me to save
Her erring child from cruel grave.
Believe her creed, as in the past,
And all your sorrows end at last
			In sweet repose."
It was an awful moment this—
Peace, safety, and eternal bliss,
			In place these woes.
Only one moment wrestled with the tempting bait;
For now she thought of all the brother's hate,
Engendered by the use of creeds—
Can ne'er supply the soul's deep needs.
But turning to the holy father said—
May I not have one crumb of bread—
The cup contains the blood He shed?
Shook now his frame; tears in his eyes—
(Oh what a spectacle for the skies),
While human pity throbbed his heart,
Gladly would he give her a part,
			The Holy Sacrament.
Alas! my child, the Church gives only those
Believes her creed, her doctrine knows.
Held out his hand, which Vesta took;
Washed with her tears, while grateful look,
Of reverent worship lit her face—
Hallowed and glorified the place.
Fast fell his tears, upon her stricken head,
As these two hearts together bled—

Gave courage to the friends of man;
Broken was bigotry's chain.
For as a ray of light from heaven's throne,
Fell on those tears, around them shone,
A light made jewel of each tear,
Set in a crown earth's children wear.
Now as the jailor came to prepare,
The execution scene, no one was there.
But as the girdle he arranged,
The knife was in her left side plunged.
Not straight, diagonally near the heart,
The touch so slight, ne'er felt the smart.
Good Friday, dawned a day of death.
Palsied her form, stifled her breath,
As first the gallows, she now saw;
Grim executioner of the law.
But now with joy, the cross she spied—
In fervent praise to heaven she cried.
'Twas by the gallows platform placed,
So kneeling down, her arms now traced
The cross-beams—her pale face,
Pressed now against its splintered sides.
And in a low despairing cry—
Seemed it must reach the throne on high;
Angels in wonder, looking on—
Men's hearts as hard as flinty stone,
Exclaimed with those stricken as she—
My God! My God! Why hast forsaken me?
A low strong voice, heard near her side;
     Spake manly pride—
" No love, I've not forsaken thee;
All's ready, darling, come to me—
My ships, my trusted men are here;

See, as before, thy great deliverer!"
Thrilling with joy, she opened her eyes;
Like Grecian god come from the skies—
            So King Alpasha stood!
To save her from this fate had come,
To place her on a lawful throne.
            As once had wooed.
From hateful death of criminal vile;
From this dreadful funeral pile;
What born of flesh could help but flee—
To Love, Light, Life, and Liberty.
 It was an awful moment for the race,
With intense interest watched her face—
            Three worlds!
Oh! she was of the spirit born;
And on this glorious tragic morn,
Won back the prize that Eve had lost—
Won, though it was at fearful cost.
Closed eyes of flesh, she looked to heaven,
Soul, with unutterable anguish riven—
Clung to the cross, with firmer hold,
As to the listening worlds she told;—
            "I can't do wrong!"
            Infallibility!!
Strength for the weak, victory for strong.
For earth what possibility.
But the heart, in its wild throb—
Determined efforts to be free—
Beat with such force against the artery,
Lies near as rent in twain,
            She's calm again.
For through the cut, the jailor's knife
            Spirited the life-blood out.

Another victim now she saw,
Came here, to pay the penalty of the law.
This man, a brother's blood had shed,
In passion dread.
By his side the holy father walked,
With holy sacrament he had brought
Unction, with sacramental bread,
With love to crown his shaven head.
Now, as the murderer took the cup,
                Looking up—
Saw how the dying woman's longing eyes
Were fixed on this symbolic sacrifice.
Exclaimed, while pity filled his soul;
Pray take, and this shall make thee whole.
As held the cup in blood stained hands,
Vesta in frozen horror stands,
For in that awful moment had took in,
Blood shed o'er earth, through brother's sin.
Another cry of dread despair,
Rang out, upon the morning air.
He held the glass before his face,
She saw him not, but through the blood
                Shed for the race
Before her, not the slayer, but the Saviour stood,
Joyful she took, and thankful drank,
No more from sinful brother shrank.
The All-Mother now besought the Son—
Go to the rescue of the stricken one,
                Spake He.
Has she not often prayed to Me?
Give her my cup; let share my cross,
Counting earth's prizes as but dross.
Shall I rob aught, her well earned prize,

The power to help earth's sons to rise
From out the slough of earth's despond—
So purer faith may now be found?
She has shown faith to trust the unseen,
E'en though in garb of vile and mean.
Can she hold out unto the end,
Save her betrayer—friend?
'Twas now men saw with great amaze
Vesta 'pon Brutus turned her face,
Surged through her heart pity divine;
While from the lawyers' damning crime
Was born twin angels, faith and love;
Sat on her now, sweet heavenly doves.
Gave him the cup, with pathos said,
" This blood our Elder Brother shed,
Shall full atonement make for sin,
Everlasting righteousness bring in."
Now heaven's light did on him shine—
He saw the woman all divine.
Standing in presence of the throng,
Proclaimed her innocence, told all the wrong.
The dead mans letter now did read.
Alpasha, giving earnest heed—
     Drew now his sword,
With all-scathing word :
" Vile wretch, betrayer of thy friend,
To hell your worthless soul I'll send!"
As Vesta saw, with one hand on the cross,
With other drew the betrayer to the side
From Alpasha's swinging sword to hide.
Mahomedan steel fell from his nerveless hand;
Sword, bare the crescent through all lands—
     A trophy of the cross!

Justice must yield to love, he said,
In lowly reverence bowed his head.
The watching angels shouted now for joy,
The tested gold had no alloy.
Jesus with rapturous love exclaimed—
(Spell-bound the people stood ashamed)
" Worthy is she, my chosen Bride,
To have a seat by my right side."
And 'fore the consecrated cross there fell
The men had fought on side of hell.
Now in the spirit saw they heaven's King!
Coming in power, his Bride to bring
Unto the wedding feast alone—
The banner in his hand was love,
And on his brow the triple-crown.
As Vesta saw her Lord, so long been gone,
Thrilled every nerve with welcome sweet;
But thought first of the sinner at her feet.
" Oh save him, Jesus, save him for my sake!"
These were the greeting words she spake.
While men in wonder stood around—
Awe-stricken fear, fell to the ground.
" It is enough," the Master said—
With matchless grace placed on her head,
Took from his brow the triple-crown;
Standing in presense heaven's throng,
    Declared her right upon the throne.
For greater was her love, than mine,
Shewed her the man behind the crime.
The bread to my betrayer given,
    Sent him to death—
Her's sent to life and heaven,
Because with woman's faith she gave

It was love's sacrament to save.
These are the greater works I promised you,
Believers in my name should shew.
Now clouds of sense were gathered o'er,
They saw with spirit sight no more.
But with a thrill of wondrous glow,
As sparks from dying embers show;
Went out the spark of Vesta's life,
Gave up the last of sense's strife.
So on a wave of joy she crossed
The river of life that men call death;
So many here are tempest-tossed,
While struggles hard this life for breath.
But here, as fades the light of day,
Sweetly her breath took leave its clay.
Now as the bridegroom's friend, Alpasha said:
I claim the first kiss from the dead.
So as she's gone to live in heaven,
This clay to Mohammedans is given.
The Holy Sepulchre she now shall share,
As she the triple crown doth wear.
He bore her form unto the ship,
Was waiting at the harbor slip.
Now weeping women standing on the shore,
Begged for a token; they would see no more.
To these Alpasha gave the heart,
So that each world should share a part,
That body broken thus for men—
All through her Christ-like love of them;
Sure pledge all hate shall be dethroned.
With Arabian spices now embalmed,
Was wafted towards the rising sun;
Sign the New Dispensation was begun.

In this Dispensation pure and sweet,
All men as brothers do each other greet.
And all religions drawn together meet
Around one common mercy seat.
Jesus, the Prophet, Saviour, King—
All tribes and nations gladly sing.
Vesta, the Priestess, Mother, Friend—
A helping hand to all doth lend.
He of the East, She of the West,
Uniting what in each is best,
Now sailing for the Eastern World.
Earth saw a banner new unfurled—

Sis.—Well, now, these verses beat all I ever seen. You can't, for the life on ye, tell when one's alive or dead. I don't know whether that woman's dead or not.

L.—It is evident, the Poet don't believe in death. Like nature, the Poet knows nothing but change of form. Life is immortal. Injury to its outward organism may cause it to leave that form, but life cannot *die*. It goes to take new form as it leaves the old.

S.—These verses would be well enough, if they were only true. But what substance is there in a picture? What is there to build on?

L.—What is nature's phenomena but a panorama which dissolves and changes even as one beholds it?

H.—Our friend thinks this would be all right if real. Now can I assure him, that instead of in any wise being an exaggeration of truth, it gives but a faint idea of the truth of woman's love, donation and sacrifice for the son of man. And who can tell the number of those, have died clinging to the cross? The nature of love is self-giving.

S.—Well, it looks as though the woman was more anxious about her enemies than friends. The only reward Alpasha got for his love and help, was a chance to kiss her after she was dead, while her betrayer was the object of very tender solicitude and devotion.

L.—A striking proof of the truth of the theory of the attractive power of love, being greatest, as the ratio of distance increases. Besides such love as his, is its own reward. No man should want pay for loving such as she.

CANTO XIX.

P.—Hark! the glad symphony—Shouts of great victory
Hail the world's jubilee—Hail Immortality.
Hallelujah, 't is done. God and Man are now One;
      Dear Father and Son—
 Faith conquers sight. Ends here the night.
 Shines now the light. Reigns now the right.
 Sis.—We don't want no more of that 'till you git some music fit for it.
 P.—Now in the Free Republic of the West
See the fair likeness John saw first—
Clothed with the sun—Light, Education,
Moon under feet. Darkness, Ignorance.
A crown of stars. The starry flag—
Tri-colored robe. Red, White and Blue—
 Liberty. Equality. Fraternity.
 Faith. Hope. Charity.
In this fair land see the home temple rise,
Where daily incense wafted to the skies—
Is loving ministry to the child.
Emanuel, God with us, shall prove
The wisdom of creating love.
O'er every cradle hear the angels sing;
While earth her choicest gifts doth bring.
Oh happy day of human birth—
      Heaven greeting earth.
 Unto you a child is born; a son is given;
Clothed with the dust, but heir of heaven.

(144)

In every coffin, weeping love two angels spies ;
In shining garments pointing to the skies.
Chanting in joyous, happy strain,
He is not here, he's risen—lives again ;
Nature's glad resurrection psalm.

Now as I, the Poet, did hear the echo of this new glad song, I saw the Lord, and his Bride did come to the Enchanted Isles ; and he did breathe upon the dry bones had lain there for centuries. And lo! they did stand up a mighty people.

Now when the Sirene Queen did hear their shouts of joy that they were men again, a mortal chill did seize upon her, and she fell to the earth as one dead.

Then did the Son and his Bride restore her to life, and when they did throw the true light upon her, her voice was restored. So doth she now sing the old songs of enchantment sweeter than before. But when she lures men to her side, she doth make them gods instead of swine.

And I saw that wherever the Lord and his Bride went, did death and hell give up their dead. And all the people were saved from their sins.

For it came to pass as soon as one was saved, at once did join the order of the Luminous Key, like that the Bride did wear, and on the band of the Triple Crown each did wear in honor of the one the Lord did take from his brow and put upon the head of his Bride were the letters in shining light: A. C. H. The Equator did circle the whole band. Now was this a secret society in that none but God knew who did belong to it. It had no outward form, but did exist under every form, concealed was this circle in every heart. And when the light of the Luminous Key did fall upon it, men could see it.

Now it was that the seed the Son and his Bride had put into the heart of Science had sprang up a new life. So that again they come to where the friends were and did beckon them to follow them. And I saw as the Bride did wave her left hand to the friends, it had on the forefinger the wedding ring of seven diamonds. And the light fell bright upon the friends.

H.—Surely, the light and union is what Socrates told the world would certainly come. The blending of all religion in living glory. It is also the fulfilling the law of Moses—love. The light of Confucius shows that the father and mother of the flesh (ancestors) are in the present world.

S.—Well, my friends, since this is something experimental within reach of all—

Sis.—I should say so, if it has come to that ; the right hand is an angel, and the left hand another. And anybody that can put their hands together can pray for the salvation of the world. Who can't do that, 'cept their hands are gone ?

W.—The heart will answer every purpose in that case.

S.—Well, as I was going to remark, the subjects treated here are practical, embraced in the inductive plan. I would like to know how I can know God.

P.—By knowing Man. What is Man ? A Trinity of Life, Will, Form. What is God ? A Trinity of Life, Will, Form. The difference is one of degree. As the life germ contains all the vital possibilities of the full grown man (although no difference can be seen between this and the plant or animal), so doth the being of man contain all the vital possibilities of God—the one the First Cause, the other the Ultimate Cause of all things.

Sis.—I never knowed God had form before.

S.—If He lacked Form, he could not be Infinite, because the lowest development of life hath form.

P.—As I see God, it is as Man multiplied to Infinity. Each of the bioplasts counting billions in the body of man, answers to the billions of souls, have lived on this earth, living active beings in the body of God. The planets are the corpuscles of his blood. The sun, his breath. The material world, the result of his thought. The living world, atoms from his Infinite Being. Life is his breath. Beauty, his form. Sound, his noise. Music, his song. Prayer, his delight.

Sis.—I don't see the good that prayer does to God. It is for us, not Him, that prayer is.

P.—It is also His delight, because it brings Him into sweet union with His offspring. Only in Man can God be seen in his entire Being. And here only in the germ. All else are but parts of the Infinite One.

Sis.—Pray, tell us what them three letters L.—L.—G. mean, at the beginning of yon picture.

P.—Law—Life—God. The Law is the means by which Life is generated. God is love, the reason why Life exists.

CANTO XX.

Now I saw that again Religion did enter the circle, and hold out her hands to Science, as at the first. Again did Science hesitate, and seemed afraid to take her offered hands. But when Sis. did give him such a look of hopeless sorrow—the pathos of childish fear, mingled with woman's despair, it did so touch his heart that he did now put his right hand into her left, while Religion did put her right hand into his left. Thus was now made an immovable foundation for the world's faith, hope and knowledge.

For a season the friends were in the same state of mind as the two disciples that were with Jesus on the mount. And in the new light that shone upon these persons they became transfigured, and to the joy and surprise of themselves and their freinds,—Tom and Eva were disclosed to each other.

It was the moment of all time, for this blighted, darkened, struggling, suffering race. God revealed in the form of man and woman—the man holding the key of all Knowledge and Wisdom, the woman of all Virtue and Love.

And these two were one;—bone of one bone, flesh of one flesh, spirit of one spirit.

Sis was the first of the number that could speak, the rest were in a world where speech has given place to a more perfect, though subtle means of intercommunion. She was in very good humor with Science, because she felt that he had taken the hands of Religion to please her, so she smiled as she said:

"Well, if you had knowed who 'twas you wouldn't been quite so crankey 'bout taken hold on her, when she come to us first."

It was enough for Science, or Tom, that he had got Religion or Eva ("what's in a name"), and he made no reply to Sis' raillery. While all the rest were so enraptured at the thought of the new possibilities for the race, this disclosure had opened up to them, they could only wonder and adore in silence. For they could now see man as the inheritor of all things. The universe was his, while the old distinction between matter and spirit, soul and body, were more clearly defined and strongly marked than ever. The location of each was entirely changed.

The material can not exist without the immaterial, for it is the life of it. And nothing exists without life. And nothing exists without place.

While the friends were so enjoying themselves and all creation, I, the Poet, did try to gather up and condense the result of all their pictures and discussion.

It looked to me as though the universe were a trinity of spirit, substance, space, as Tom said at first. I called it S. S. S. Then it was I saw what Eva did; that only through sin could sinners be saved from sin. For there could be no such thing as holiness without sin. Sin being the transgression of a higher law in honor of a lower one. So I put sin saves sinners right under spirit substance space, and bound the double S. S.'s together with a chain called experiment or induction, and let the people, by aid of this key, make out life's problems.

To confess the truth, I was tired of discussion and study. I wanted to enjoy Tom and Eva. He was asking a question, and I thought more of hearing the answer than anything else, because her action in leaving him just as he had married her had been the great puzzle of their history.

Being still in the flesh, and not having any lost aim through which she could talk to me, I could not understand her language. But I saw how his face lit up; and when she had done speaking he clasped her to his heart (you can see people even when you can't understand their language), exclaiming: " And so through all time and eternity I will have a Virgin Bride."

Poetry and Law did clasp hands, as Science and Religion had done. But when Wisdom offered hers to Sis., she drew back, saying:

" No, friends; 't aint no use. I've did what I could for the world, but my day is past. In the New Light of the present I should look ugly and disagreeable. If I was cross and selfish when I first came here, 'twas 'cause I thought you was trien to git the blessed Jesus 'way from me. But I do declare you gi'n him better and better every day to me.

Once he seemed to me like a great king, pitied me like a shot bird, or a crushed worm. Now he is my own big brother. I know he'll never let anything hurt me. He'll always take care of his own little Sissy. That's enough for me."

Now as she spake thus, I saw the light of the Bride fall upon her.

Lo! now did the wrinkles transform themselves into lines of ineffable Beauty. Out of this transfigured form shone the sweet childish face of her men had so despised and called Ignorance.

And it came to pass as she receded from her old friends, she threw to each a kiss, which each returned, while Wisdom exclaimed—

" Bless the sweet cherub. Why surely there never could have been such a thing as moral virtue, Divine, Man and Womanhood, without her " (S. S. S.).

Now, so delighted was Science with his long, lost bride, thus truly his forever, that he gave the children of men a glass upon which could be photographed the invisible Body, Faith had so long believed in. Looking into this glass was seen the invisable world that is covered by the outer. Composed of the same atoms, (as Spirit, Substance, Space). The invisible life was to this, what the light is to the lump of coal in which it is imprisoned till freed by combustion. I saw as the light of the Bride fell upon this glass, that Doubt and Despair—the devils—had been Tom's companions since his youth, receded into the darkness of the past, and were seen no more.

Born of the night, they dissolved in the light of the New Day; henceforth to live only in the glorified consciousness of their old time victims.

Now did the glory of God and Man so fill the whole world, that in its light I saw their bodies as a transparent veil for the inner being. And I saw all birds, animals and fishes, as the Truth and Law incarnated in Life and Form. And all phenomena as the law and will of the Supreme One, whereof each seperate *one* was a part.

Manifest to our senses as Creator, Preserver and Destroyer; to our minds as Law, Justice and Truth; to our souls as Righteousness, Purity and Love; to our hearts as Father, Mother, Son.

And now could man truly enter upon and into his rightful inheritance as the supreme force in Nature. This watery veil called body looked like the vapor out of which the rainbow is formed, the nebula out of which new marvels are continually created.

And I heard the music of the spheres, the songs of the blest. And they chanted and sang, while all the inhabitants of the Glorified Earth joined in the chorus:

Glory to God in the highest!	Glory to Man in the lowest!
Almighty Father!	All Conquering Son!
All Loving Mother of MAN.	All Beautiful Daughter of GOD.

THE WORKING PEOPLE.

To the Pastors of the Churches in Milwaukee and Bay View.

Rev. Fathers and Brothers:

We come seeking your help in a matter of vital interest to all. We entreat you, that you look not upon our request for special prayers as Mr. Tyndal's request was received. We believe that his request was made in the interest of a more certain knowledge, something that could be known of the laws that govern the most important and vital function of soul-growth and Christian work. There seems to be a great lack here. The promises that we are asked to believe in seem too much like the old currency, that was a promise to pay at nowhere and no time. A striking example of the confusion and uncertainty that reigns here was shown in the prayers for Garfield. As this old fiat money has been wisely displaced by a foundation of solid gold, so we desire to see the promises laid down in the Holy Bible brought into the realm of law, that we may obey, and thus reap the benefit. For we cannot but see that the gulf between the working people and the Christian church is growing wider and wider. Things are rapidly tending to the same condition as Dickens and Gough found in London. As they went among the poorer classes, the one for material for his books, the other for his lectures, they found that religion had come to be looked upon as an ornament for the rich, with which they had nothing to do. Deeply do we deplore this, for we fully believe that any real good to us as men and women, or as working people, must come on the lines of light and truth, pointed out by our Brother, the Carpenter of Nazareth. We are told that He has left this work, and makes known His will to you. So it is that we come to tell you our needs and seek help to lift us out of the mire and dust of our daily toil, into the pure light of truth and beauty. Many of us are compelled to work so hard that we be more like beasts of burden than like Sons and Daughters of a King. Perhaps this hard life makes the clear light of faith, that shines upon you, impossible to us. We need something that is real and certain that can be depended upon every time. Now if prayer is such a power, we want to know it. It must be capable of proof. We know that through the laws of sound, the power concealed in the belfry of one of your churches may affect the air of the city, and by this means reach every ear. Now what we want to know is, if there be a law corresponding to this, by which, in the circles of prayer inside the churches, your people can draw from the heart and life of God, and send new life out to reach our hearts, and affect our minds as the sound of your bells does our ears?

We know that thought is electric force, and you say it is spiritual as well. We know that electric force is as capable of transmission as sound. Now we ask if you may not send out your thoughts to us, freighted with the truth of God, laden with the feeling of love and hope that you enjoy? Your creeds we poorly understand, but that ignorance does not prevent our ears from hearing your bells, need it keep our hearts from feeling your love, our souls from feeling your life? In the interests of Man, we beg a practical test, that we may find the law of prayer. Will you, and your people, at the hour of morning devotion, Catholics at the morning mass, at 2 o'clock P. M., at 8:30 P. M., concentrate your thoughts upon God, and the great mass of outsiders who have not your light, that thus you may become the medium through which our Father can reach the hearts of His children, and do them good.

If prayer is as sure as the forces of attraction and repulsion, the thought of God and Heaven would be borne to the toiling mother as she bends to her daily task, it would come to the child in the school, louder than the din of machinery will the voice of God be heard in the workshops and marts of trade. Then would the empty seats in your churches soon be filled, and your hearts made glad by the cry, " the dead's alive, the lost is found." We entreat and implore that you consider our request, pray over it and grant it for Christ's sake.

WORKING PEOPLE.

THE WORKING PEOPLE'S PRAYER TEST.

The words of " Luca " in the Herald have the ring of the true metal. They show an honest desire to find the truth shall unite the people as brothers in a common good for all men. But we trust our new found friend will not " go back on us " because we say " thought is electric force." We live at the bottom of things, and dig at stern realities. In our " off-spells " of work we study the problems of life in books and people. We take the facts we thus glean back to the furnaces, and in our hearts and brains they are puddled and baked over, heated and reheated till they have a new appearance.

All that is not essential to the truth, all the errors have gathered around it, we try to let go out of it, as the sweat takes off the effete particles from our systems. Now when we find that " every thought, every feeling, has its definite mechanical correlative," etc., the materialists tell us these facts prove their position. We dump them all together in the hot fires of experience, work them over and over. And thus we find that they do certainly prove the first postulate of religion. So do these facts bring us face to face with an Omni-present God, manifest in every atom. They do also show us a law by which a man's feelings for his " best girl," his sorrow for sin ; his faith and worship can be gauged-tested and used as certainly as any other force in Nature.

Endowed with this power, we feel ourselves masters of the situation. So do we now gladly come on to the platform " Luca " invites us on, to test this power as it is manifest in prayer. We take God for our Father, Man for our brother.

First we find a life force that takes the food we eat, bread and water, etc., and converts it into a living body capable of thought and feeling. The Catholic Church embodies and celebrates this great mystery with all its higher meanings in the service of the Mass. Now suppose that at morning Mass, as Father Fagan pronounces the words that crystalizes and reveals this great fact—the transformation of common material things into the divine—bread transformed into a living Christ offered to every person in Bay View. Suppose that in the supreme moment of consecration as the words " this is my body " go out on the morning air, the thought of each worshipper should take it as the air takes the sound of the bell and bear it to the mills and homes. Would not the people be thus led up from the groaser, earthy fact of their lives to its higher meaning in Divine Sonship? Would not the Catholic Church thus get her reward for her faithfulness in holding on to this truth through all the darkness of the past? Try it, friends ; try it.

Another great law is that of the stronger force overcoming the weaker. Is not the God in men the strongest element of life? There be many in Bay View who fully believe it is. Some of these unite together, concentrate their thought upon those who have need to grow into the knowledge of their Sonship with Christ. At 2 o'clock P. M. they make special effort to draw from the life of God the power that shall open the eyes of all such, that they may have will to come to the light. " Luca " plainly shows, quoting from Christ, that the fault is in the will. But of all the people *who willed* to take that " fatal train," how many would have so willed had they known what is now known? So it is certain that could all men know sin as some know it, the *will* would lead them from it. Could they all see Christ as some see him, he would, as he says, "draw the hearts of all men " to their Father and

Brother. To the certain force thus brought to bear upon them through the medium of prayer, there be plenty of living witnesses in the mills and homes of Bay View. To some it has come with such power as to sober them in the extreme of intoxication. To others a saving power to overcome the evil of their natures. The little that has been done is enough to warrant the conclusion that if all would concentrate their mind force every day at 2 P. M. in a persistent, determined effort to bring the children and the All-Parent into a closer union, where the life of the Infinite could flow into and stimulate the lesser life of the child, many more would be able to rejoice in God and rest in the arms of Peace and Love. In behalf of the "weary and heavy laden," we beg the friends of all to try it. Surely, there be none but can " give a thought." Another great truth is the *unity of man*, shown in the creed of the workingmen : " An injury to one is an injury to all." Now suppose that at the hour of meeting for the different unions the men whose hearts are burdened wlth this great truth, were to fix their thought upon those who fail to see and feel it as they do, as Jesus did when he said, "inasmuch as ye did it to the least ye did it unto me." Suppose those who feel with Christ, the full force of this central truth of humanity, were to unite and send the truth out on the lines of thought and waves of feeling that envelop and surround them and their neighbors. It is so easy to propagate scarlet fever and diphtheria that our board of health orders the red and blue cards. Is it any less easy to propagate life and love than disease and death ?

We should like to see the experiment tried. We should like to see every union man with a label that should tell all he met that in his heart there was burning a fire that will certainly burn out this old order of " Selfish Monopoly," and bring in the reign of " Brotherly Love." At 8:30 P. M. most of the lodges have their meetings. Why not give five minutes to earnest thought; silent prayer (if the words are not a stumbling block), to the carrying of their feeling to the hearts of those who have it not. It couldn't be lost time. Try it, friends. Give it the benefit of your strong brain and heart power, and see if even your indifferent neighbors don't wake up to new life of love for all. "Luca" thinks our first appeal ought not to have been made to the pastors of churches. Perhaps not. Possibly they are not as "remiss in duty" as we are. Let us, then, fearlessly do for ourselves what they can not do for us.

Rev. L. N. Wheeler, in the pulpit of the M. E. Church, spoke of the blowing up of Hell Gate in New York Harbor, when the touch of a little girl, on the electric wires, caused the final overthrow. Thus, said he, are the gates of hell, honeycombed with centuries of work, filled with the giant powder, awaiting only the touch of faithful prayer to realize the truth of the promise, "the gates of hell shall not prevail against you." Shall that touch of power that shall overthrow the kingdom of darkness come from the working people of Bay View?

Last year rang the death knell of the "Labor Riots" through all the world. Shall not 1887 ring out the glad tidings of the New Life?

PRAYING BANDS

Hold Cottage meetings at the homes of the people every Tuesday evening.

YOUNG MEN'S BAND

Meets every Friday evening.

PRIZE ESSAY.

THE LOVES AND FISHES.

Man's first want is air. He lives on air, while he lives, and when he can no longer appropriate the air he dies. A great deal of fun has been expended on the happy lovers who live on air. But as Victor Hugo declared they were the only true philosophers in the universe; so modern science is demonstrating they are the greatest discovery in the universe. How much wiser to spend the day like the turtle dove, billing and cooing, making ones self and everybody else as happy as can be; than to be sweating over a hot furnace or steaming over a cook stove till one is so tired the ugly devil comes out spontaneously. The only trouble is to keep him back. "But," says one, bound by the darkness and ignorance of the past, "this sort of thing don't get a living." Now, this is just the sort of thing that should get a living. Man was not made to be a mule, or a machine. In the air, in the sunlight, is the supply of his bodily wants. The wise Persian saw in the sun also the brightest image of God. Be it so. The material and immaterial are now found to be inseparable. The one cannot exist without the other. Science confirms the old insight of faith, and finding life everywhere, in every atom, confirms and establishes the "omnipresence of God." But, says one when these spooney lovers come out of the seventh heaven, where they live on honeymoon, they find they must work for a living like other folks. Well, that is just the trouble with them. They should stay in the higher realm of being and not come down into the world of toil, contention and strife. They loose the secret of condensing food, fuel and happiness from air and sunlight, when they come on to this low plane. Just so did the world lose the secret, from the time of Moses and the prophets to the time of Christ. Moses was learned in oll the wisdom of the Egyptians. And what command they had over the elements is shown by the monuments of the Nile, as well as attested by the records of both sacred and profane history. And in the various tests to which Moses was subject with the wise men, how he always exceeded them. And when he came to have an immense people to feed in a desert where nothing could grow, he showed how food could be condensed directly from the elements, without the bloody process of the past. Food that must be secured at such an outlay of toil becomes red with human blood. Now, as refined steel is made direct from the crude iron instead of the old process of puddling, so should food be condensed direct from the elements. Let us take the loaves and fishes, bread or meat. Now, by subjecting this to electric processes of heat, it can at once be reduced to the elements that compose it. Let any housewife throw a piece of meat on the coals and see how quickly it goes off into the air whence it came at first Now, should the chemist do this In a glass tube. Here are the elements that was in the meat or bread. Now should he experiment with it until he can condense it again in some form? The Jews seemed to get tired of this food, aud sighed for the leeks and onions of Egypt. But I see no reason why science should not by this proeess give us the leeks and onions as well as the manna. Perhaps they might not have such a disagreeable odor. So also in producing wine from the water. Science should study carefully all the details of the historic accouut. Every element that goes into the pure juice of the grape should be added and this subjected to electric process. But it is said that we have no evidence of the manner in which electricity was used in the recorded cases of developing food and wine direct from the elements. It is very likely that this force was evolved from the brains of the people. Thought is the epitome of all power and force. It is material, as can be tested in experiment. It is also spiritual, as can be proved by the phenomena of all conscious intelligence. In each of the five thousand fed by Jesus, was a condensing engine, so to speak, the power of which, modern science, with all its boasts, can but feebly imitate. But the cost of developing electricity through the brain will eventually prevent this process in our day of machinery. Electricity can be produced so much cheaper now. These things seem to have been written for our inspiration and guidance rather than to give details. The record of the 'loaves and fishes' direct our attention to the rich provisions in the bosom of nature for all our wants of body and soul. The Catholic Church claims the same power that has always existed, to do the works of God. Surely with science as her servant she ought now to feed the starving millions in her fold, as her Lord fed them. Protestants assert the universal rigor of law. If this thing has been done for forty years' why not now?

Question for the Independent Literary society, Milwaukee:

Resolved, That it is the prerogative of man to draw food and fuel direct from the sun. The HERALD will furnish leaders for the affirmative if desired.

THE IMMORTALS.

Ruskin says the world has sat at the feet of poets, philosophers and scientists; has been governed by Kings, Emperors, Priests and republicans, and has not grown any better. The only hope is, therefore, in the working people. This poem is written in the confidence that those people are living in Bay View. And, that when the "coming man" gets here, we shall see him shod with hob-nails, and with a white towel around his neck. However, if this coat fits any person who wears blacked boots, and keeps his towel hung on a peg, he has the right to put it on.

Hark! now they come, who herald the day,
The dawning day of happiness.
See! now they come who open the way,
The glorious way of righteousness.

Here are the ones who carry the light,
The light of the new dispensation.
The ire's the force that will drive out the night,
The night of man's degradation.

This is the royal manhood true,
Wearing the garb of the working man,
Come to ring out the old, ring in the new,
Come to destroy all glittering sham.

And in their stead, enthrone the right,
Set up the Kingdoms of man.
Reveal to Earth the glorious light
Hidden since time began.

* * * * * * *

All hail, immortal working men,
All hail! ye true and brave,
Stronger are ye than all have been
Go forth, the weak to save.

Sound now the call to battle, that shall never know defeat;
Begin the march to glory, that shall never know retreat;
The world has long been waiting for you;
Ruskin, the men you seek are in Bay View.

THE HERALD'S EASTER GREETINGS.

Hail! this light morn the gladdest day that has ever dawned on earth, for now has science wrested the key from the hand of nature and man may enter into her store house, eat, drink and be merry. Now can be heard the voice of the son of man sounding through the troubled waters of labor and capital, saying "come unto me, all ye that labor and are heavy laden, and I will give you rest." How will he give us rest? By supplying our wants. Through the magic touch of electric force, the flowing waters of earth shall be turned into wine, to gladden the heart and nourish the body. Moses, took water and threw it on the land and it became blood. So do we. In the slow, laborious process through which we draw wine and bread from the bosom of nature, it becomes poisoned by the " worm of the still," it becomes red with the blood of the toiling millions of farmers, railroad men and toiling women whose lives are spent in this service.

Our brother, Jesus, showed us that the pure wine could be made direct from the water. He showed us that bread and meat could be developed direct from the elements of which they are formed, without the old bloody process of toil and sweat. He pointed to the law that would remove the curse of toil that ignorance and disobedience had laid upon man. He showed us how men should live as sons and daughters of the living God, not as beasts of burden. He showed how man should love his brother. It is not for one set of men, (capitalists), to grind all the work they can out of the laborers while he combines with others to keep the non-union men in starvation, but because of ignorance and unbelief we have said that we could not walk in the path he marked out. We can not have the mastery over the elements He declared is the heritage of man. We can not live drinking the wine of gladness, rejoicing over our work. There is naught but the old bloody way of the past.

Shame! on such weakness. Shame! on the world that has chained the lightening to its wires, that has annihilated space, that has outwitted time and sends its message ahead of the clocks, that warms itself by natural gas and beats the sun by its electric light. And now it can't find that the law by which the demands of life may be satisfied without the toil that makes life a curse, "not worth the living." Oh! science and civilization, ye have done much for man, but except you do more you and we had better have never been born. If we must work like beasts to supply the demands of the body, why force upon us the developed train, the sensitive nerves of manhood ? But worse than this, you have invented machinery to take our places and now we must starve for want of the work we perhaps might better die than do. Have ye no bread to offer but must be red with our brothers' blood ? You have multiplied our wants until our scanty wages are but as a drop of water to our parched tongues. Cease now your proud boasts of what you have done for man. Go into the wilderness of want and hunger with our brother Jesus and there with him wrest from nature the secret by which water is made wine, and air and light are made bread and meat. You have every advantage in discovering this secret. Electricity, chemistry and biology, are well known to you. Feed us with the living bread from nature's overflowing storehouse or we perish with hunger. Give us the new wine of the kingdom of man; happiness, knowledge, virtue and brotherly love, or we die of this consuming thirst. Make the opening greeting true history or mankind will curse you. God help you.

APPENDIX.

WHO WANTS MORE LIGHT?

Liberty's light went out. The woman's light has gone out. Why? The light of the one was hidden in coal, the other is hidden in words, and there is no money to pay the miner or the printer. The woman was to stand at the gateway of the "New World" to show the "way to the tree of life," that all might eat and live forever. She takes the place of the "angel with the flaming sword," to keep man out of Paradise. Could the light shine, would the darkness comprehend it? Perhaps not. I have little hopes that the truths set forth in these pages will have much offect, until the world shall have been purified by fire.

But such parts of the book as I have been able to pay for (about one third of its pages) are sent out as a witness of a higher law of being than man has known. If there be those who desire to more of these truths, be it known that one hundred and twenty-five dollars will pay for the first one thousand copies, when it could be furnished for $50 per thousand. Past

Since the above was in type, I have received as a Christmas present the money necessary to complete a press edition, from a husband whose love of the writer doth so exceed his contempt of the writing. And now in this effort, to place Religion on the sure foundation of Science, I have a right to claim the help of the Press.

Brave Knights of the Pen!! Help the woman lift the world to the Light. The Old, has a man with a world on his back. The New, has a woman with a world on her breast, giving a new life.

Know ye not, oh men of the press, ye represent the God incarnate in words as does the Pulpit in worship.

"THE WORD WAS GOD."

I was in advance of Tyndall in advocating a prayer test. This book is the result of experiments continued through twenty-five years. Instead of being a work of inimagination, as Mr. Ingersoll thought, it is the vital outgrowth of facts of people I have known; which have been recorded in a journal, the first date being May 2 th, 1862. Having found (by the test of induction) the truth, I was prepared to unite with my fellow working people here, and urge upon all the necessity of seeking to find the laws of growth in the higher life. Some friends think this work is born fifty years to soon. " Earning our bread by the sweat of our brow," we have no use for our money except to glorify man. So such as we can afford to wait. The best use could be made with the money put into this work, was to give employment to others. So it can be no loss. Working people should be as anxious to *give* jobs as to *get* them. We give a few extracts from out home paper, the *Bay View Herald*, to show what we are trying to do. If it be thought by any, that we are in any wise able to help in the uplifting of the race, we can furnish books or papers at the cost of labor and material. Duties are ours. Results are with God.

BAY VIEW

HERALD.

"MAN IS LOVE"

OPINIONS OF THE PRESS:

As light and darkness go together and good and evil are linked by Inseparable bonds, we put the two together in our selection of the many opinions of the Press called forth by the first publication of this work.

"As a work of fiction this story has decided merit. The life of rich and poor, pro- and anti-slavery families, is well sketched, and sketched, we are pleased to say, with manifest independence of French and English models —[Wis. J. of Ed., Gen. Fallows, editor.

"A semi-philosophical novel of some interest, the work of an active but unbalanced mind, full of visionary thoughts, etc.—[N. Y. Independent.

." Paul, Paul, thou art beside thyself. Much learning doth make thee mad."—Felix.

The authors' name is not given. He merely styles himself as one who knows, or thinks that he knows that "Man is Love," in which case he is happier than some of his fellows, whose experience leads them to think differently. Portions of the work are excellent and indicate riginal ihought, etc.—[Eve. Tel., Phila.

"The author of "Man is Love," sets out to prove that human nature is not so bad as represented, but on the contrary, is at bottom noble, even adorable, and her reasoning is plausible—contains food for serious reflection. Darwin's ask is mere play compared to the painstaking abor of this author.—[Detroit Post.

"The story is not above the average. However, whatever opinion the public may form regarding the work, the author has no disturbing doubts on the question.—[Sat Eve. Gaz., Boston.

What the Greek youths did and endured for Hellen's sake, men will be ready to do, in different forms, for beautiful women, etc. Our enthusiasm for this new regime is somewhat depressed by the extremely long time we must wait. This golden age can only come when woman's nature is so developed that her smiles and frowns are the reflections of infinite love —[N. Y. Home Jour.

There are sentences which have the exquisite charm of Lambs Rosemond Grey. The book is of much interest and we hope to hear from the writer in a second volume.—[N. Y. Even'g Mail.

Eva, the heroine, and her lover, Tom, have some passages of sentiment and experience in life which entirely redeem them from commonplace romance, two characters well worth study.—[Philadelphia Age.

Could not have been written before this age, a pioneer in the christian and philosophical plane of love, unfolds a new theory of love as the power of God in the world, has a mission in the world, some passages surprise one by their power and spiritual insight.—[Living Way, Cal.

There are many interesting passages, but the movement is not rapid;—on the whole the book is well worth reading.—[St. Louis Rep.

The absurd title of an American story.—[N. Y. Herald.

The poorest thing about the book is the title, it has decided felicity of diction and absurdity of idea, slave and child features of much interest, dialect quite good.—[N. Y. Even'g Mail.

To point out what we regard as its serious and pestilential errors, takes more time than we can give to it.—[St. Louis A.

A story of varied incident in which children, men and women are depicted as in life. In all of us there is something of the Divine, some germ at least of that the sacred writers meant when they said God is love.—[Washington Daily Chron.

"Our moralist says " not the sword or the ballot is to govern the world in the future.—Woman's smiles and frown will be the chief good, the most terrible curse.

The title, vague as it is excentric, affords no clue to the contents of this book. The story is told in a way quite independent of classical models—with freshness and vigor of delineation —inculcates a sort of optimist philosophy based on the inailenable right of every human being to be loved and thought well of.—[N. O. Times.

The best part of Man is Love is the preface, in which the author undertakes to prove the fitness of the title—some gems of gold—does not pay to search through its 470 pages to find them.—[Literary World.

Man is Love is the startling proposition of a Southern authoress. We wish for the sake of humanity, she had been more successful in proving her theory. Some may find it interesting, we confess we are not of that number. —[Theadore Tilton's Golden Age.

Of Man is Love, it may be said, if the preface is a representative of the bill of fare, it must be good reading for subject and moral alike The author is evidently in earnest in writing and rather confident than otherwise, of original deserts to be recognized.—[Bos. Times.

Told in a sermonizing way, American life is faithfully depicted —[Eagle Press.

OPINIONS OF THE PEOPLE.

Mrs. M. C,. ex-president of W. C. T. U. "I have tried some of your theories and Oh! what a heaven it makes of home. The book is full of capital things and crowded with thinking."

I wouldn't give the thing house room. W.

My husband never read a book that did him so much good. Wife.

There is no head or tail to it. W.

Reading that book to my wife I had to follow wherever her work called her, when she was washing I had to tune up loud. Farmer.

Oh! that blessed book, when will you write another? I have lived so much of it that I know it is true. Miss.

I sat up nearly all night to read it. Mother.

I should say, part hog. part bear, part aligator, with a little sprinkling of angel thrown in for yeast. Capt.

"Man is Love." I am on that platform.
H. W. Beecher.

Handsomely bound, price $1.75.—[Press.

NOTE.—Canto 13, page 85. A woman in the Milwaukee House of
rrection was gagged according to law for singing on a Sabbath evening.
reports.

ERRATUM.

For "Copyrighted by Herald Publishing Co.," read "Bulah Brinton & Son."

CUT OF ROLLING MILLS.

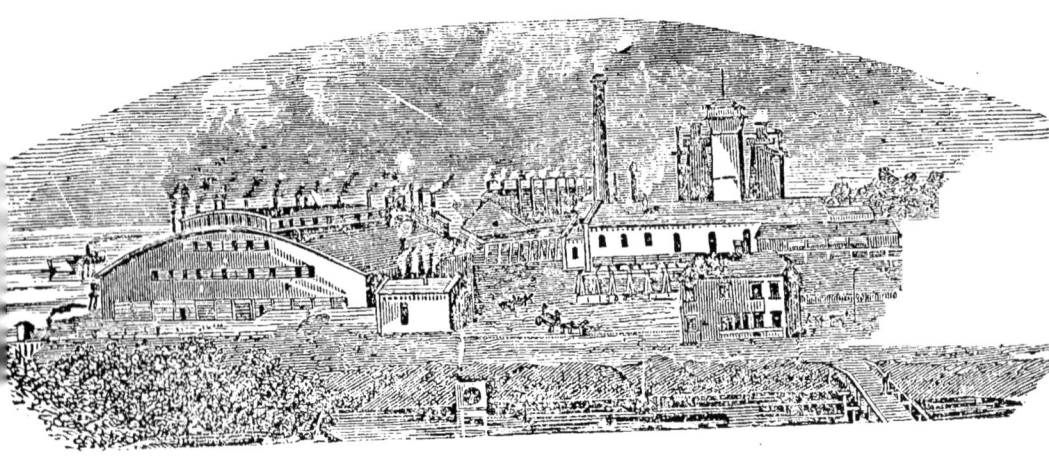

Mills closed by labor troubles, May, 1886.

INDEX.

	PAGES.
CANTO 1—THE POET'S STORY,	1–5
2—THE NEW LIGHT,	6–7
3—MARRIAGE OF THE SON,	8–11
4—TOM'S STORY,	12–21
5—THE FIVE FRIENDS.	22–45
6—THE FIVE FRIENDS—Continued,	46–50
7—SCIENCE REFUSES RELIGION,	51–55
8—WOMAN OF THE WEST,	56–60
9—BIRTH OF THE SON,	61–62
10—WOMAN OF THE WEST—Continued,	63–72
11—SATAN'S WOOING,	73–80
12— " " Continued,	80–84
13— " " "	85–90
14—	91–100
15—	101–108
16—	109–119
17— " "	120–126
18—	127–143
19—	144–147
20— "	148–151
THE WORKING PEOPLE,	152–154
THE WORKING PEOPLE'S PRAYER TEST,	155–158
PRIZE ESSAY,	159–161
THE IMMORTALS,	162–163
THE HERALD'S EASTER GREETINGS,	164–165
APPENDIX,	166–172

Capt. E. B. WARD, founder of Bay View.

Sample home of a day wage-worker in the employ of the North Chicago Rolling Mill Co., Bay View.